Psychology *of* Option Trading

Psychology *of* Option Trading

MAHESH CHANDRA KAUSHIK

PRABHAT
PRAKASHAN

Published by

PRABHAT PRAKASHAN PVT. LTD.
4/19 Asaf Ali Road,
New Delhi-110002 (INDIA)
e-mail: prabhatbooks@gmail.com

ISBN 978-93-5562-820-6
PSYCHOLOGY OF OPTION TRADING
by *Mahesh Chandra Kaushik*

Edition
2025

Price
₹ 300 (Rupees Three Hundred Only)

Printed at
Siddhi Press, Delhi

Author's Note

Dear readers,

Greetings!

My second book written on options trading has reached you. My first book on option trading 'How to Grow a Tree of Money with Option Trading?' was so appreciated by readers that it has currently become the best seller in the segment of option trading among the books written on the Indian stock market.

I received requests from many readers who loved the first book that I should also bring out a book on advanced methods of option trading so that they can earn a regular monthly income by adopting other new methods like the tree of money method.

At the time of writing this book, it has been assumed that you already have a basic knowledge of options trading and you are already familiar with the terms like Call, Put, Option Chain, Strike Price, Call Writing, Put Writing, Option Selling, Expiry, Bid Price, Ask Price, etc. In case you do not have this initial knowledge, then before reading this book about advanced methods, you should read my first book 'How to Plant a Money Tree Through Option Trading?' in order to get the basic information.

Generally speaking, there is a tendency in people that they want to achieve everything without working hard. It is due to this tendency that people invest in the stock market without reading any books about it and without doing any hard work. They invest directly based on hearsay and advice of friends. When they lose their entire capital, they curse the stock market, future trading and option trading all their life.

In options trading, you can make money ten times faster than buying and selling ordinary shares. But the opposite is equally true, that is, you can lose money ten times faster.

For example, if one person rides a motorcycle at a speed of 20 kilometres per hour and another person rides a motorcycle at ten times that speed, i.e. 200 kilometres per hour, then who do you think has more chances of meeting with an accident?

Naturally, your answer will be that the second person is more likely to have an accident than the first one. Therefore, you should not jump straight into options trading if you are totally new to the field. First, you should work in the cash segment of the stock market for at least 3 years. After that, you can start option trading based on this book. That is, after gaining an experience of driving a motorcycle at a speed of 20 to 80 kilometres per hour for 3 years, you can qualify for the initial ability to drive a motorcycle at a speed of 200 kilometres per hour.

The above statement is also not completely accurate. Suppose, you ride a motorcycle at a speed of 200 kilometres per hour on the street of your locality. For one, motorcycles these days do not reach speed of up to 200 kilometres per hour. Therefore, first, you will have to buy a Ninja bike worth ₹ 15-20 lakhs that can be driven at a speed of 200 kilometres per hour. However, if you drive it on the street of your locality at a speed of 200 kilometres per hour, you are sure to go to heaven (die).

This example of a bike is exactly applicable to options trading. That is, first of all, you should opt for option trading only if you have a minimum capital of ₹ 15-20 lakhs. Second, you cannot ride a ninja bike at a speed of 200 kilometres per hour on the local streets and it will require a racing track. Similarly, first, you should read the first part of this book titled 'How to Plant a Tree of Money Through Option Trading?' and prepare a racing track by planting one money tree each in Nifty and Bank Nifty. Then you will be ready to earn/lose money ten times faster with options trading.

You bought the book. But you cannot learn options trading just by buying the book. If you are really serious about making money and trading options, you must read the book in its entirety.

From my experience, I have seen that 80 percent of readers just buy the book. Then they read a few chapters in the beginning, a few pages in the middle, some part of the end of the book and keep it aside.

As I always say, earning money and working hard - both work in equal proportion, that is, if you want to earn money, you also have to work hard. Here, the only effort that you have to make is that you should not just buy the book and keep it on a shelf at home. Rather you should read each and every page of the book carefully and then gradually translate the principles mentioned in it into reality.

I also ask you not to think of trading as an investment that gives fixed returns like the bank FD. Investing and trading are two different concepts. There can be both profit and loss in trading. Therefore, the principles for building your mental maturity for options trading and managing position size that are outlined in the early chapters of this book are essential parts of the book. You are expected to acquire sufficient mental maturity for trading first by carefully reading and following the introductory chapters. Then ensure that you limit the position you would take according to the position size, and avoid being avaricious and taking over positions under any circumstances.

I have not written this book to earn royalties from my readers. My aim for writing this book is that it should benefit millions of traders doing option trading and that they should avoid huge and immense losses in options and become successful traders instead of wasting money in the name of trading.

After you read this book, you should gain experience in all the principles I have told you by paper trading for at least a month. You should get into real trading after that. Paper trading means taking an imaginary position instead of the actual position, noting it on paper and noting down the imaginary profit-loss on paper according to the stop loss hit or booking profit.

Paper trading for one month is the best real time back test. This will give you a good idea of the stop loss by reviewing your position every 15 minutes.

But, in today's world of ChatGPT and AI (Artificial Intelligence), we do not want to work hard. We are busy watching statuses, reels, videos on our mobiles and keep wasting our time. Then we think that we would get the data of back test, etc. readymade from somewhere so that we can avoid the hard work of the paper trade.

Before I begin writing this book, I would like to express my gratitude to those people, without whose blessings and guidance it would not have been possible for me to write the book. First of all, I would like to express my gratitude to Supreme God who is the Creator and Operator of his world, who chose me as His medium in this mortal world and selected me to spread the knowledge of investing in the stock market through me.

I would like to express my gratitude to the most revered Bal Naga Sanyasi Shri Sahadev Giriji Maharaj, who took the place of my Guru after my Guruji Shri Shri 1008 Satyanarayan Dasji Falahari Baba left this world, and enfolded me in the embrace of his love and filled the void left by my Guruji's departure.

I am grateful to my wife, Mrs. Seema Kaushik, who supported me in every aspect of life. She never stopped me from taking risks in the stock market, due to which I was able to move forward in every aspect of life with the loving support of my wife.

Finally, I am grateful to my 2.25 lakh YouTube followers because it was only with the constant appreciation and encouragement from my followers that I was able to clear the NISM exam and become an SEBI Registered Research Analyst.

So, now you can start reading the book and using the principles stated in the book, become a successful options trader and begin earning a regular monthly income.

– Mahesh Chandra Kaushik

Assistant Revenue Accounts Officer

Collector Office, Sirohi

(NISM Certified and SEBI Registered Research Analyst)

Contents

Author's Note 5

1. Are You Mature Enough for Options Trading? 13

2. Trade Only in Index Using Advanced Methods of Options Trading 19

3. How to Reduce Margin Money for Option Writing? 24

4. How to Get Regular Monthly Income from Short Straddle? 27

5. What is the Difference Between Straddle and Strangle? 42

6. How Did the Share Genius Short Strangle Method Help Earn 12 Percent Monthly Returns? 46

7. Qualities of a Successful Options Trader 53

8. The Owl Short Strangle Method 60

9. Do Not Change Methods Frequently in Options Trading 72

10. Can One Get More Reliable Data Than NSE? 77

11. What is the Iron Condor Strategy? 82

12. My Scales Method for Options Trading 95

13. How to Earn Regular Monthly Income by Selling Covered Calls? 102

14. Sell Share Genius Covered Calls Instead of Poor Man's Covered Calls 110

15. Experiences of Some of My Readers About the Methods Described in This Book 119

16. How to Sell Gold and Silver Covered Calls for Option Trading in Commodities 125

17. Earning Regular Income from Options Trading in the Forex Market 128

18. Vertical Strangle Method 135

19. Summary 142

1

Are You Mature Enough for Options Trading?

Recently, I went to a shoe shop to buy shoes for my son. As soon as I entered the shop, three people present in the shop (one of whom was the owner of the shop and two were his friends) were extremely happy to see me. They seemed like a hungry man who becomes elated after getting food.

They quickly ran towards me. Their behaviour stunned me. It seemed to me as if that day they had not sold even a single pair of shoes and that they would make sure to sell me many of them. The three men animatedly said, "Are you the one who has a channel based on stock market on YouTube?"

I said, "Yes, I am the same Mahesh Chandra Kaushik."

Then they started praising me, "Sir has also written many books."

I asked, "Have you read my books, too?"

They replied, "Oh, who has time to do that?"

I looked around their entire shop. There was no customer there except me. So, I couldn't understand why they didn't have time to read books. Well, overall, after adequate hospitality, they said that they do option trading, and so, if I told them about any of the shares, they would buy its call or put and would be grateful to me.

I politely refused and said that I would not tell them about any such share before leaving from there. The shopkeeper and his friends thought that since I was also a trader, I would not give them tips for options trading for free. So, they said, "Sir, don't worry, we will pay your fees." Upon hearing this, I explained to him, "It is not a matter of fees. I do not charge any fees for my advice. But you do not seem mature enough to me for option trading. Therefore, in case I suggest a stock for option trading to you and for some reason that stock does not perform as per my prediction, then the next time I pass your shop, you will hit me with a shoe instead of welcoming me."

When they heard what I said, all three of them felt bad and their faces fell. So, I started explaining to them to mollify them. I asked them, "How long has it been since you people opened a demat account?" In response to this question, someone said that it was 2 months, someone said it was 3 months and someone else said it was 5 months. I explained to them, "If someone wants to obtain a driving license, he has to get a learner's license first, that is, he has to learn to drive an ordinary car or jeep. One also has to practice for at least 6 months, and after learning to drive the vehicle for 6 months with a learner's license, the person gets a driving license. Then how is it possible for you to gain the high-level knowledge of trading practices like option trading on your own with just 2-4-5 months of experience?"

In fact, such new traders keep shooting in the dark. Sometimes they earn ₹ 5,000-10,000 and the next day they lose ₹ 20,000-30,000. Overall, these people continue to incur losses.

So, my first rule of thumb before getting into options trading is that for at least 1 year, you must regularly do delivery-based trade in the cash segment of the stock market.

To trade in the cash segment of the market, you should divide your total capital into 40 parts and work in the cash market for at least 1 year using the principles explained in my books 'You can also become an intelligent investor' and '41 trading tips'.

This will give you an adequate idea of how the stock market operates. Suppose, Ramu opens a demat account during the bull run of the market. He observes that the market was at 14,000 (Nifty 50 level in April 2021) and it went up to 17,000 (Nifty 50 level in September 2021) within 4-5 months. Now during these 4-5 months, he will form an impression that the stock market always goes up and hence it is beneficial to make bullish deals. With this assumption, Ramu starts option trading. After some time, the market falls from 18,000 to 16,000.

Therefore, if Ramu had traded in cash for at least a year, he would have gained sufficient experience. He would have seen a rise of 14,000 to 17,000 and a decline to 18,000 to 16,000 in the market.

So, my first rule of thumb for gaining enough maturity for option trading is that you should have at least one year of experience in the cash segment of the stock market.

Now, let us talk about the second rule. I have spoken about this rule many times before. The rule is that if after one year you have earned at least 12 percent net annual return on your total capital in the stock market, then only can it be said that you have gained enough experience.

Suppose, you started trading by investing ₹ 4 lakhs in the cash segment of the stock market and after one year your total profit was only ₹ 20,000 or you suffered a loss of ₹ 15,000 to 20,000, then it means that you are still not mature enough for options trading. In fact, a return of ₹ 20,000 on a capital of ₹ 4 lakh is only 5 percent, which indicates your immaturity because you could have earned more than this, i.e. 6-7 percent in a bank FD. If you have got negative returns or incurred losses, then it is a sign of even greater immaturity.

Therefore, watch my videos or trade in the cash segment based on my books, and first reach at least a level where you start booking profits over 12 percent per annum from the cash market even if it takes more than a year.

Now, you might ask - what if you earn 12 percent profit in the first month itself? Even if you have earned high returns in less than a year, you are not yet mature because the market may have been bullish at that time. Therefore, you will not gain maturity unless you also go through a period of decline. Hence, even if you have earned more than 12 percent returns in less than a year, you must wait for at least one year.

Now the next rule to get into option trading is – 'Availability of adequate capital.' According to me, to do option trading successfully, you should have at least ₹ 15 lakh of self-earned extra money.

When I say 'self-earned', it means that the amount is completely yours and you do not have to pay any interest etc. on it. I receive dozens of e-mails where people say - Sir, I have lost my entire money in option trading. Now, I am nervous. I am not able to eat. I feel dizzy. I am also worried about the future of my children. Now, you are my only hope. Please do not disappoint me, do respond to my e-mail. I have lost my entire capital. But I will take loan from my father for whatever trade you suggest. My father has just received his retirement fund.

I respond to such e-mails, too. I tell them – I am sorry, I do not have any magical tips by which you can recover your lost money, and you should never make a mistake of doing option trading with your father's money. Now you should go for swing trade in the cash market and forget about the options market for some time. That is why I chose two words – first, 'self-earned', that is, if you have your own money and not the money of your parents, friends or from bank loan, then you have acquired the ability to do option trading.

The second word that I have written is 'extra money', that is, you should not need this money for the next 2 years for children's future, marriage, house, education etc. Only then will you be able to take risk on this amount. Otherwise, you will get nervous midway and start making mistakes. So, overall, to work in option trading, you must have three basic qualifications, which in short are as follows –

1. At least a year's experience of working in stock market.
2. Ability to earn at least 12 percent returns annually by trading in the cash segment of the stock market.
3. Self-earned extra amount of at least ₹ 15 lakh.

So, in a nutshell, I would ask you to acquire the above-mentioned qualifications before you start trading with the help of my advanced methods in the option trading segment of the stock market so that you do not face failure in option trading.

There is no need to be disheartened or discouraged in case you do not have the above three qualifications. If you practise my swing trading methods of cash segment, you will easily learn to earn 12 percent annually and if you continue practising my money tree method in option trading - both Nifty and Bank Nifty – based on my first book on option trading 'How to plant a money tree through option trading?', then gradually your total capital will also keep increasing.

Another option is that you can assimilate the methods mentioned in the book by practising paper trading. After gaining enough experience, you can gradually convert it into real trading and learn to earn regular monthly income from option trading.

❑

2

Trade Only in Index Using Advanced Methods of Options Trading

In this chapter, I will explain the advanced methods of options trading, which you should use only for trading indices – i.e. Nifty, Bank Nifty or Fin Nifty (Nifty Financial).

This is because about 80 percent of the trading in the options market takes place in indices and the remaining 20 percent of trading takes place in stocks. Therefore, there are substantial volumes at different levels in the index. The real thrill in creating and selling positions in options is only when there are enough buyers/sellers available at your desired strike price. Hence, in index, when there is sufficient availability of both buyers and sellers at most of the strike prices, trading can take place more easily.

Apart from this, there is no big unexpected movement in the index together. Therefore, your chances of making money are more in this. On the other hand, if you make a position in a particular stock, and there is an appreciable rise or fall in the stock in the opposite direction than your expectation, then you are sure to lose your entire money.

In case of most new options traders, once they make big money on a position, they become addicted to it. It is actually a psychological process - whatever gives us pleasure or makes us feel happy leads to the creation of dopamine receptors in our brain for that particular thing.

It is only because of these dopamine receptors that people become addicted to alcohol, sex, drugs, sweets, bidis-cigarettes, gambling, lottery, betting, etc. so that they feel the same pleasure again.

Similarly, winning money in a lottery or online cricket app creates dopamine receptors in the human brain, which make him addicted to buying lotteries again and again or playing games in apps with financial risk again and again. In the same way, when you earn money in option trading a few times, dopamine receptors are formed in your brain. As a result, even though you know that your chances of earning money next time are less, you continue to create positions in options blindly.

I have seen the majority of option traders in the market losing their entire capital due to this addiction. If you lose your capital in option trading, then neither the option market is to be blamed nor the person who taught you the option trading strategy is to be blamed. In fact, it is your greed, your fear and your habit of creating large positions in a hurry to win at a spur of emotions are fully responsible.

For example—I teach you to drive a car. But it is entirely up to you whether you follow the driving rules and complete the journey and reach your destination or whether you drive recklessly and risk your life and that of others.

Yet another example is of electricity. Either you can make your life comfortable by using the appliances that run on electricity or you can die by touching bare electrical wires. Therefore, before proceeding further in the book, I would like to tell you that all the methods mentioned in the book do not guarantee 100 per cent success. But it is certain that if you have gained the experience described in the first chapter and have learned to recognize market trades, then you will definitely earn money overall using these methods. Because if it were not possible to earn money from option trading, then so many strategies would not have been invented.

Therefore, you should keep these points in mind while using these methods so that you can earn money from them-

1. Trading options in indexes is safer than trading in specific stocks. So, use the methods in this book for trading in index.
2. Do not trade in options for pleasure and thrill like one finds in addiction to alcohol, gambling or betting. After carrying out thorough analysis, create small positions thoughtfully while keeping in mind that the position can also go against you. So, do not hesitate even if you have to book a loss occasionally.
3. Do not fall into the trap of doubling your money in option trading. I have seen many new traders losing their entire capital in the options market. When I talked to these traders, I found that in 90 percent of the cases, when these new traders got double the return on their capital, they started trading ₹ 40,000 to ₹ 80,000, then ₹ 1,60,000, then ₹ 3,20,000, then ₹ 6,40,000, then ₹ 12,80,000, then ₹ 25,60,000, then ₹ 51,20,000, then ₹ 1,02,40,000 – this means that they were trading with an impossible target of making ₹ 1 crore from ₹ 40,000 in just 8 trades.

During your childhood, you must have learnt in school that greed is evil. This proverb is equally relevant in option trading, too. Therefore, do not fall into the trap of earning quick money in just 8-10 trades. Keeping in mind that you have to earn from the option market throughout your life, you should take small trades wisely and sensibly and not wait till expiry in option trades. My experience is that except Iron Condor, you should never hold any option position overnight and whatever profit or loss occurs, you should book it in intraday only.

In this context, let me share with you an amusing story. There is a child in my neighbourhood. When he is asked to count from 1 to 20, he counts as follows – 1, 2, 3, 5, 10, 15, 16, 17, 14, 20.

Now if that child is told that he has counted incorrectly, he insists that he was correct in counting. I believe that the child is correct in his counting from the perspective of the stock market because there are gap-up and gap-down openings in the stock market. Here, if a share closes at ₹ 10, it is not necessary that the next day it will start trading at ₹ 10 or ₹ 11. The next day that share can directly open at ₹ 8. This is called 'gap-down opening'.

Similarly, if a share closed at ₹ 10, it may directly open at ₹ 12 the next day. This is called 'gap-up opening'. Due to these gap-up and gap-down openings, a small investor can get badly trapped in an option position. Therefore, in all the methods that I propose to teach you in this book, I will advise you to book profit/loss in intraday. The reason is that by creating a new position every day, you have a forecast of the direction of the market for that day. Secondly, you are able to avoid huge losses in gap-up and gap-down openings.

No matter how much stop loss you set, your stop loss is not triggered in gap-up and gap-down. Suppose, you bought a call option at ₹ 153 and your stop loss is ₹ 140 and this call closes at

₹ 149. You hold this position overnight. Unfortunately, the next day, if this call opens directly at 128, then your stop loss of 140 will not be triggered and you will incur a great loss.

I have met many ill-fated option traders who fell prey to similar gap-ups and gap-downs, and thus lost most of their capital in large overnight positions. As a result, they gave up options trading completely.

There is another example of this. Ramlal books profit-loss in Nifty 50 position in intraday. He sometimes books a profit of ₹ 500, sometimes ₹ 700 and sometimes ₹ 1,000 on one position. He also has to book a loss sometimes. Thus, by regularly booking small profits and small losses, he books a total profit of ₹ 15,000 and loss of ₹ 5,000 at the end of the month. So, after deducting the loss, his earning for the whole month was ₹ 10,000.

On the other hand, Shyamlal holds the position of option till expiry and books a profit of ₹ 6,000. So, in spite of this, Ramlal's profit remains higher. On the other hand, there are also chances of Shyamlal incurring a loss if he holds for the whole month. So overall, the essence is that we have to use advanced methods of option trading to trade in the index. We have to trade only in intraday by taking small positions after analyzing the direction of the market. However, I will also mention some methods like Iron Condor in which you can hold till expiry and then trade.

One advantage of index trading is that settlement of index options is in cash. Apart from index, all other stock options are settled through physical delivery. Hence, since index has cash settlement, you do not need to keep an additional margin or shares for physical delivery.

❑

3

How to Reduce Margin Money for Option Writing?

When you sell an ATM call of an index option, you require around ₹ 1 to ₹ 1.25 lakh of margin money per call-put. Most small investors do not have that kind of margin money. Therefore, they buy call-puts instead of selling them because only premium has to be paid for buying call-puts. Therefore, because of a low margin, small investors buy call-puts in this low margin.

But have you heard about the concept of the 'Max Paine Theory'? In case you do not know about the Max Pain Theory, then let me tell you about it. According to this theory, big traders know how many option contracts have been bought and sold and at which strike prices. Therefore, they try to ensure that the options are settled till expiry in such a way that most of the option contracts expire worthlessly (without getting any profit).

What this means is that the option buyers get maximum (max) pain. That is why it is called 'Max Pain Theory'. In other words, it can also be said that the structure of the option market is such that by holding it till expiry, the contacts of most of the option buyers expire worthlessly (without getting any profit).

Therefore, according to the Max Payne Theory, option writers, i.e., those who sell options, are always in a position to earn more than those who buy options. Therefore, most of the advanced strategies about which you will learn in this book will use option selling. Now you think that this would require a lot of margin money.

But if you hedge your position, that is, create two or more positions in such a way that if there is a loss in one, there is a possibility of profit in the other position, then you have hedged your position. Now the exchange knows that you are less likely to suffer a loss in a hedged position. Therefore, the exchange does not levy high margins on hedged positions.

For example, if you sell a Nifty ATM call, you need a margin of around ₹ 1 lakh. Likewise, if you sell one ATM put on Nifty then you require margin money of around ₹ 1 lakh.

Now, if you sell 1 ATM call-put each together, then you will need a margin of more than ₹ 2 lakhs for both together. But this is not how it happens. Actually, by selling call-put together, your position is hedged. Therefore, now the margin required is less than selling call-put alone, i.e. around ₹ 90-98,000.

Thus, because of the hedge position in most of the methods described to you in this book, you will need less margin than normal. To meet this margin, you do not need to have full cash. You need to have 50 percent margin in cash, and you can keep the remaining 50 percent margin as collateral margin.

Here, collateral margin means that you can maintain this collateral margin by pledging the shares or units of ETF that you already hold. However, brokers charge interest at the annual rate of 9 to 12 percent on this collateral margin that you obtain by pledging shares. Therefore, I would recommend you to adhere to cash margin only. If you have planted a money tree as per my first book and you want a margin on your hold units, then you can obtain the margin by keeping them as collateral at the annual interest of about 12 percent and opt for option selling.

Basically, margin money depends entirely on the potential loss you incur. In the following chapters, you will get to read about my Iron Condor strategy, in which 4 positions are created simultaneously. That means, you sell 1 call, buy 1 OTM call with the premium received from the same and sell 1 put, and then buy 1 OTM put with the premium received from the same. When you create 4 positions in this way, the possibility of loss is appreciably reduced, hence the margin payable by you also reduces and comes to only ₹ 50-60,000.

❑

4

How to Get Regular Monthly Income from Short Straddle?

The first of my advanced methods of options trading that I propose to explain to you is the Short Straddle method. This is a type of hedge position. In this method, two positions with the same expiry at the strike price are created in such a way that in one position, there is profit if the market falls and in the other position, there is profit if the market rises.

1. Long Straddle
2. Short Straddle

In long straddle, call-put of the same strike price are purchased together. Long straddle is profitable only when there is a huge movement in the market in any one direction. This type of straddle is more profitable only when there is a big event, for example, on the day the budget is announced, the day when the election results are announced, etc.

Generally, it is not possible to see large moves in the market every day. Therefore, if you use the long straddle continuously for a long period of time, it is generally less likely to be profitable.

For example, on March 3, 2023, the Nifty opened at 17,451.25. Accordingly, if we buy a call-put together at the nearest strike price of ₹ 17,450, it becomes a long straddle. Now let us see what results we would have had if we had made such a long straddle in intraday on March 3, 2023? For this, we will use data of open and close price for back-test. On March 3, 2023, the call of 17,450 opened at 218.95. That is, if you had bought it as soon as the market opened, you would have bought it for approximately ₹ 218.95. On this day, there was a major move in the market and the Nifty closed at 17,594.35. So, by the time the market closed, the call of 17,450 closed at 330.45.

So theoretically, on a call of ₹ 17,450 taken at this open price, you would have made a profit of approximately ₹ 330.45-218.95=111.50 per share and on a lot of 50 of Nifty, the profit would have been ₹ 5,575. Now, on the contrary, let us look at the result of the trade, in which you would have bought a put of ₹ 17,450 to create a long straddle. Its open price on March 3, 2023 was 193.35 and close price was 115.90, which means you would have incurred a loss of ₹ 77.45 per share. Since there was a lot of Nifty 50, your overall loss on this trade would have been ₹ 3,872.50. Overall, you would have made a profit of ₹ 5,575 and incurred a loss of ₹ 3,872.50 in this long straddle and during of the closure of the market, you would have made an intraday profit of ₹ 1,702.50.

But on this day the market closed at 272.45 points (1.57 percent) higher than its previous close, so you benefited from the long straddle. Long straddle in intraday is profitable only when there is a simultaneous movement of at least 1 to 1.50 percent in the market.

The market does not rise by 1 to 1.50 percent every day during the entire month. So, if you use long straddle in intraday every day for the entire month, you will make a profit when there is a big move on 4-5 days of the month and the day when there is less movement in the market, you will incur a loss. As a result, overall, you will incur a loss in the whole month.

Therefore, always remember that long straddles, in which you buy call-puts of the same strike price at the same time, cannot be used continuously in intraday to earn regular monthly income.

Long straddle closes on profit only in 5-7 trading sessions in a month. In the remaining 12-15 trading sessions, the long straddle closes on loss. Here, we are talking about making a long straddle in intraday. I do not recommend making long straddles for the whole month or the whole week because if the market remains range bound, your premium on both sides will go to waste and you will incur immense losses.

Every day in intraday, by making a long straddle trade in the first half hour around the open price and closing the profit or loss in the last half hour around the close price, the entire month's premium does not go waste even in a range bound market. Rather, sometimes there is loss and sometimes profit and still some premium remains.

Now, if the market is in a bull run and there is a daily fluctuation of more than 1-1.5 percent in the market for most of the days of the month, or even in a bear run market, there are big fluctuations in the market for most of the days of the month, then it is possible that you may get a profit in long straddle in that month. But long straddle is not very effective for earning regular monthly income.

Overall, this book will not teach you how to make money with the long straddle because the long straddle is not an advanced option trading strategy. This is a common strategy, which is profitable only if there is a move of 1 to 1.5 percent in a month. In this chapter, you will be taught about how to earn from short straddle. I have already uploaded the video of this method on my YouTube channel. That is why many of my followers earn a regular monthly income with my simple strategy of short straddle. First, let me explain to you the theory of how this short straddle is made. I have posted this method on my YouTube channel with the title 'How to earn around 10 percent monthly income from option trading in intraday'. You can also watch my YouTube video related to this by searching this title on Google/YouTube.

The name of this method is 'Open Selling'. Therefore, in this, you have to make a short straddle by selling 1 call-put each together around the open price. Now you will ask why 1 call-put each. It will be less exciting. I sell approximately 10 lots together, only then it becomes more exciting.

Here, my request is that even if you have more money, do not sell more than 1 lot because this is not the end of the book. I am going to tell you many about such methods in this book. If you have more money, then you can also use those methods.

Now, in this method my followers also have a doubt that how is it possible to sell at open price? In options, prices change very rapidly. So, how can we sell as soon as they are opened? You are absolutely right. Here, I am not talking about selling as soon as it opens. Open price means the open price of Nifty, which we use for selecting the strike price. That means, in this Share Genius Open Selling Short Straddle, whatever At The Money call (ATM call) is based on the open price of Nifty, we sell calls of the same strike price and sell puts of the same strike price for which we have sold the call.

Now, if you wanted to make an open selling straddle on December 30, 2022, then on this day i.e., December 30, 2022, you would see that the open price of Nifty was 18,259.10. This means that the call of the strike price of 18,250 is an ATM call. So, you had to sell 1-1 call-put of strike price ₹ 18,250. Now, the next question is that 'When should it have been sold?' So, the answer is that it was to be sold in the first half hour after the market opened.

With this trade, you will benefit from time decay that occurs in premium throughout the day. As you know, premiums decrease over time. Secondly, no matter which direction the market moves, your premium will increase on one trade and decrease on the other trade. You should have covered this trade with whatever profit you made or loss you incurred in the last half hour after the overall market closed. Now you have sold the call-put before, so buying it back would mean - covering it.

In this method, you get the maximum benefit during those months when there are no major fluctuations in the market. The only way that we can check this method with historical data is to assume that we have sold a call-put around the open price and covered it around the close price.

When you use it in practice, you will see that you cannot just sell at the open price or at the close price. There will definitely be a difference between them. But by checking this method on the basis of open-close prices from historical data, you can make a rough estimate of its performance.

Accordingly, if you had sold a call-put of ₹ 18,250 together based on the market open price of ₹ 18,259.10 on December 30, 2022, you would have received a premium of approximately ₹ 306.10 on the call of ₹ 18,250. Actually, the 18,250-call opened at 306.10 on March 30, 2022. I suppose it is true that you could not hold it at 306.10. But it is possible that you could have taken a premium over ₹ 306.10 in the first half hour, but it also could have been slightly less than this.

Overall, this would not make much difference to our calculations because if you had got a premium of less than ₹ 306.10 on a call, then you would have got a higher premium on a put almost equal to the same amount. You already know that when you short call-put, their premiums move opposite to each other.

Because only if the market had fallen after opening, you would have got less premium on your call. However, in case of the market falling, the premium you get on the put would have increased. Therefore, the result of the open and close price of call-put based on the back-test historical data that we are going to bring will be almost similar to real-time practical back-test.

On December 30, 2022, the market came down and closed at 18,105.30. Therefore, around the close price, the premium of ₹ 18,250 call had reduced from ₹ 306.10 to ₹ 241.05. Nifty has a lot of 50. Therefore, in this trade you would have made a profit of ₹ 65.05 per Nifty share. Multiplying this by 50 would have earned you a profit of ₹ 3,252.50 per lot.

Now, naturally if you have made a profit in the call trade then you will suffer a loss in the put trade. In the put trade of December 30, 2022, the premium for short selling at the open price was ₹ 255 and the premium for covering the position was ₹ 289.80. That means you incurred a loss of ₹ 34.80 per share (per Nifty) and of ₹ 1,740 on a lot of 50. Now on this short straddle of selling call-put together, you made a profit of ₹ 3,252.50 and incurred a loss of ₹ 1,740. So, overall, you would have saved an overall profit of ₹ 1,512.50.

As you have already read in the previous chapter, a margin money of around ₹ 1 lakh is invested in this. Therefore, earning ₹ 1,512.50 in a day on an investment of ₹ 1 lakh can be called a very good return. But this does not at all mean that you now have a magic lamp in hand and so you will keep making short straddles and, in this way, keep earning lucrative returns.

In fact, no method of option trading is 100 per cent safe. There is no guarantee that you will make a profit from this every day. If there was a guarantee of earning through this method alone, then why would I advise you in the first chapter of this book to opt for option trading only when you have a margin money of at least ₹ 15 lakh?

In this short straddle, only about ₹ 1 lakh margin money is required to short 1-1 lot. Then why do you require ₹ 15 lakhs? Actually, there is no guarantee that you will earn daily income through any method of options trading.

I will try to explain to you on the basis of historical data of January 25, 2023 as to what would have been the results if you had made a short straddle for the entire month at the monthly expiry of Nifty of January 25, 2023.

As mentioned earlier, to estimate the back-test based on historical data, we assume that we have sold at the open price and covered the position at the close price. Even though it is not possible in practice, you can create a position around the open price in the first 30 minutes and cover around the close price in the last 30 minutes. Since the prices of call-puts move opposite to each other, overall, there is not much difference between this approximate calculation based on open-close and the real trade calculation.

The series of monthly expiry of January 25, 2023 started on December 30, 2022. Therefore, on December 30, 2022, if you had sold a call with the strike price of the Nifty's open price and covered it at the close price, then in this type of trade you would have made a profit of ₹ 14,892.50 in the entire month, which you can see in this table –

Table 1

Date	Opened	Closed	Call Sale	Premium Received	To be Paid On	Profit/Loss
30-Dec-22	18,259.1	18,105.3	18,250	306.1	241.05	3,252.5
02-Jan-23	18,131.7	18,197.45	18,100	315	351.2	-1,810
03-Jan-23	18,163.2	18,232.55	18,150	293.2	332.95	-1,987.5
04-Jan-23	18,230.65	18,042.95	18,200	291.25	191.2	5,002.5
05-Jan-23	18,101.95	17,992.15	18,100	262.9	206.15	2,837.5
06-Jan-23	18,008.05	17,859.45	18,000	252.05	186.25	3,290
09-Jan-23	17,952.55	18,101.2	17,950	255.95	330.25	-3,715
10-Jan-23	18,121.3	17,914.15	18,100	220.25	146.9	3,667.5
11-Jan-23	17,924.25	17,895.7	17,900	255.75	230.75	1,250
12-Jan-23	17,920.85	17,858.2	17,900	240.7	196.45	2,212.5
13-Jan-23	17,867.5	17,956.6	17,850	219.8	268.85	-2,452.5
16-Jan-23	18,033.15	17,894.85	18,000	210	125.8	4,210
17-Jan-23	17,922.8	18,053.3	17,900	180.65	257.9	-3,862.5
18-Jan-23	18,074.3	18,165.35	18,050	170	218.35	-2,417.5
19-Jan-23	18,119.8	18,107.85	18,100	151	116.85	1,707.5
20-Jan-23	18,115.6	18,027.65	18,100	113	70.05	2,147.5
23-Jan-23	18,118.45	18,118.55	18,100	75.3	90.3	-750
24-Jan-23	18,183.95	18,118.3	18,150	81	34.8	2,310
25-Jan-23	18,093.35	17,891.95	**No trade on expiry day**			0
Total profit of the month						**14,892.5**

Here, you will see that no trades have been taken on the day of expiry i.e., on January 25, 2023 because the premium for expiry is very low and due to high volatility of expiry, it is most likely to incur losses. So, in my methods, you are not to take any trade on the day of expiry.

Now let us look at the put trade. If from December 30, 2023, the daily put had been shorted at the open price and covered at the close, then there would have been a loss of ₹ 3,760 in the entire month as follows –

Table-2

Date	Opened	Closed	Call Sale	Premium Received	To be Paid On	Profit/Loss
30-Dec-22	18,259.1	18,105.3	18,250	255	289.8	-1,740
02-Jan-23	18,131.7	18,197.45	18,100	212.45	179.05	1,670
03-Jan-23	18,163.2	18,232.55	18,150	211.95	166.65	2,265
04-Jan-23	18,230.65	18,042.95	18,200	193.95	289.4	-4,772.5
05-Jan-23	18,101.95	17,992.15	18,100	230	241.55	-577.5
06-Jan-23	18,008.05	17,859.45	18,000	190.45	243.95	-2,675
09-Jan-23	17,952.55	18,101.2	17,950	201.65	111.8	4,492.5
10-Jan-23	18,121.3	17,914.15	18,100	168.1	263.25	-4,757.5
11-Jan-23	17,924.25	17,895.7	17,900	165.7	172.3	-330
12-Jan-23	17,920.85	17,858.2	17,900	131.9	181.65	-2,487.5
13-Jan-23	17,867.5	17,956.6	17,850	154.95	99.95	2,750
16-Jan-23	18,033.15	17,894.85	18,000	143.7	185.65	-2,097.5
17-Jan-23	17,922.8	18,053.3	17,900	137	72.95	3,202.5
18-Jan-23	18,074.3	18,165.35	18,050	122	70.2	2,590
19-Jan-23	18,119.8	18,107.85	18,100	98.5	102.7	-210
20-Jan-23	18,115.6	18,027.65	18,100	102	116.1	-705
23-Jan-23	18,118.45	18,118.55	18,100	55.15	43.8	567.5
24-Jan-23	18,183.95	18,118.3	18,150	38.65	57.55	-945
25-Jan-23	18,093.35	17,891.95	**No trade on expiry day**			0
		Total profit of the month				**-3,760**

Overall, you would have made a profit of ₹ 14,892.50-3,760=11,132.50 in the entire month.

But earning money in the options market is not so easy that you just keep making short straddles with this method and keep earning 10-12 percent returns every month.

In fact, the movement of the stock market never stays the same. Sometimes, the market continuously has a bear run and at other times it continuously moves sideways. Therefore, it is natural that no single method will consistently deliver profits in every condition of market. Now let us look at the reverse side of the short straddle method. If you had made a short straddle in intraday every day for the whole month with this method in the month of expiry of October 27, 2022, then you would have incurred a loss of approximately ₹ 11,630 by selling calls in the entire month as follows.

Loss incurred by selling call at open price and covering at close price in the month of expiry of October 27, 2022 –

Table-3

Date	Opened	Closed	Call Sale	Premium Received	To be Paid On	Profit/Loss
30-Sep-22	16,798.05	17,094.35	16,750	395	**570.15**	-8,757.5
03-Oct-22	17,102.1	16,887.35	17,100	326.8	**254.1**	3,635
04-Oct-22	17,147.45	17,274.3	17,100	325	**434.15**	-5,457.5
06-Oct-22	17,379.25	17,331.8	17,350	330	**285.95**	2,202.5
07-Oct-22	17,287.2	17,314.65	17,250	318.55	**329.7**	-557.5
10-Oct-22	17,094.35	17,241	17,050	325.9	**376.1**	-2,510
11-Oct-22	17,256.05	16,983.55	17,250	250.95	**165**	4,297.5
12-Oct-22	17,025.55	17,123.6	17,000	228	**336.7**	-5,435
13-Oct-22	17,087.35	17,014.35	17,050	280	**245.1**	1,745
14-Oct-22	17,322.3	17,185.7	17,300	200.5	**171.05**	1,472.5
17-Oct-22	17,144.8	17,311.8	17,100	300	**332.65**	-1,632.5
18-Oct-22	17,438.75	17,486.95	17,400	175.25	**236.45**	-3,060
19-Oct-22	17,568.15	17,512.25	17,550	154.95	**132.2**	1,137.5
20-Oct-22	17,423.1	17,563.95	17,400	160.15	**222.1**	-3,097.5
21-Oct-22	17,622.85	17,576.3	17,600	120	**93.3**	1,335
24-Oct-22	17,736.35	17,730.75	**Mahurat Trade option closed**			0
25-Oct-22	17,808.3	17,656.35	17,800	80	**18.95**	3,052.5
27-Oct-22	17,771.4	17,736.95	No trade on expiry day			0
Total profit/Total profit of the month						-11,630

In the above table you can see that though the share market had opened on October 24, 2022, the market was open only for one hour for *Muhurat* trading because it was the festival of Diwali. Therefore, the option market was closed on that day.

Owing to expiry on October 27, 2022, no trades are to be taken and none of my methods are to be used on the day of expiry. During my free classes on YouTube, some overenthusiastic followers ask - On the day of expiry, can we trade in the expiry of the following week or month?

I do not answer this question because the overall market is subject to change and fluctuation on the day of expiry, which impacts the expiry of any month or week.

Thus, you can see in the above table that if you had made a short straddle in intraday daily for the entire month with this method in the month of expiry of October 27, 2022, then you would have incurred a loss of approximately ₹ 11,630 upon selling calls in the entire month. On the contrary, selling the put would have resulted in a profit of only ₹ 450, which you can see in the following table –

Table-4

Date	Opened	Closed	Call Sale	Premium Received	To be Paid On	Profit/Loss
30-Sep-22	16,798.05	17,094.35	16,750	347.05	242.45	5,230
03-Oct-22	17,102.1	16,887.35	17,100	359.05	461.5	-5,122.5
04-Oct-22	17,147.45	17,274.3	17,100	300.6	241.35	2,962.5
06-Oct-22	17,379.25	17,331.8	17,350	276.1	309.4	-1,665
07-Oct-22	17,287.2	17,314.65	17,250	287.5	250.05	1,872.5
10-Oct-22	17,094.35	17,241	17,050	255.55	198.8	2,837.5
11-Oct-22	17,256.05	16,983.55	17,250	252.4	434.75	-9,117.5
12-Oct-22	17,025.55	17,123.6	17,000	251.2	226.35	1,242.5
13-Oct-22	17,087.35	17,014.35	17,050	258.55	283.05	-1,225
14-Oct-22	17,322.3	17,185.7	17,300	241.55	275.55	-1,700
17-Oct-22	17,144.8	17,311.8	17,100	197.15	132.65	3,225
18-Oct-22	17,438.75	17,486.95	17,400	169.8	136.75	1,652.5
19-Oct-22	17,568.15	17,512.25	17,550	180.05	187.4	-367.5
20-Oct-22	17,423.1	17,563.95	17,400	151.2	82.1	3455
21-Oct-22	17,622.85	17,576.3	17,600	138.45	129.75	435
24-Oct-22	17,736.35	17,730.75	**Mahurat Trade option closed**			0
25-Oct-22	17,808.3	17,656.35	17,800	95.95	161.25	-3,265
27-Oct-22	17,771.4	17,736.95	**No trade on expiry day**			0
Total profit/Total profit of the month						**450**

Therefore, as a result of your loss of ₹ 11,630 and profit of ₹ 450 in the entire month, your overall loss in the month would amount to ₹ 11,180.

However, for the expiry of October 2022, if you had made a short strangle for the entire month ('Strangle' is an improved form of Straddle, about which you will be told in the next chapter), you would have made a profit of ₹ 12,740.

Therefore, you should not make short straddles in more than 1-1 lot every day. The remaining margin has to be used in other methods taught and reviewed in this book so that on that day, if there is a loss in one method, then there is a profit in the other method and you get overall profit.

Secondly, this method is to be used only in the monthly expiry of Nifty and Bank Nifty. The third point is about stop loss. Whenever you start seeing a loss of more than ₹ 2,000 (two thousand) in any one leg of a call or put upon selling 1 lot each, then you have to cover the short straddle by covering both the call and put together.

Your total loss from this will be less than ₹ 2,000 because the call-put that you sold together move opposite to each other. That means if there is a loss in one, there is a profit in the other. Therefore, if there is a loss of ₹ 2,000 in one leg (i.e. in either call or put), then there has to be some profit in the other. So, overall, your loss for the day remains limited to below ₹ 2,000.

If the losses are limited to below ₹ 2,000 (we are talking about ₹ 2000 in either call or put and not both together) then you can square off in the last half hour of the market by holding the position.

To sum it up, trading is an art. If you practise this short straddle of intraday with the stop loss mentioned above, you will be able to make profits in most months. However, you should remember that there is no guarantee of 100 profit in any of the methods of options trading. Sometimes there are losses in trading, which is natural; even the biggest traders sometimes incur losses. In order to limit these very losses, you have been suggested above to keep a stop loss of ₹ 2,000.

Anyway, by using these methods in intraday trading, the losses are already limited as compared to holding overnight.

❑

5

What is the Difference Between Straddle and Strangle?

Now, the method which will be explained in the next chapter will be based on Short Strangle. Before proceeding further, let me clearly explain to you the difference between Straddle and Strangle.

In straddle, you buy and sell call-put together with the same strike price and the same expiry date, but in a straddle, you do not need to keep the strike price the same. That means, in straddle you simultaneously buy or sell call-put of different strike prices with the same expiry date.

Here you should note that in strangle, the options must have the same expiry date, but you can choose different strike prices. Like straddle, strangle is also of two types –

1. Long Strangle
2. Short Strangle

When call-put with different strike prices and the same expiry are bought together, it is called 'long straddle'. As I have mentioned in the previous chapter, the method for making short straddle and long straddle will not be taught here.

In this book, you will be taught different methods of making a short strangle like short straddle.

In fact, it is profitable to create a straddle when you are unsure whether the market will rise or fall. But while creating a strangle, you have a market range in mind and that the market is not likely to go above or below that range.

Now, a question arises - which is the more profitable method between straddle and strangle?

The simple answer is that if your guess about the market movement is correct, then there is more profit in strangle than in straddle. But you do not have to get confused with such questions.

My theory is simple and straightforward. In this, if you have margin money of ₹ 15 lakhs, then using the margin money of ₹ 2 lakhs, you should make a short straddle of 1-1 lot both in Nifty and Bank Nifty using Share Genius Short Straddle-1, open selling method as mentioned in the previous chapter.

In Nifty Share Genius Open Selling Straddle, you have to use monthly expiry, and in Bank Nifty, you have to use weekly expiry.

The short straddle made by selling the mentioned 1-1 lot of call-put should be made during intraday and if there is a loss of more than ₹ 2,000 in any one position of call or put, then it should be considered as stop loss and both the positions should be covered at the same time.

If this stop loss is not triggered, then both positions should be covered in the last half hour of the market.

Now out of ₹ 15 lakh margin money, about ₹ 2 lakh will be used to make 1 short straddle of Nifty-Bank Nifty each. Out of the remaining ₹ 13 lakhs, using ₹ 2 lakhs, Share Genius Short

Strangle has to be made from 1 lot each in both Nifty-Bank Nifty with the Share Genius Short Strangle method explained in the next chapter.

Incidentally, nowadays trading has started in Fin Nifty, too. If you want, you can make straddle and strangle in Fin Nifty also at different strike prices.

What I mean to say here is that in order to be successful in options trading, you should not depend on a single strategy and all positions should not be made at the same strike price, same expiry and at the same time.

The statement that I have made above is the bottom line. This may seem slightly difficult to understand and may also seem shocking to many. But let me explain it to you again.

I have written above that in order to be successful in options trading, you should not depend on a single strategy and you should not make all positions at the same strike price, same expiry and at the same time.

When you create an open selling straddle, the method for which I have described in Chapter 4, and as soon as the market opens, you immediately make a short straddle in Nifty, Bank Nifty, Fin Nifty, on the basis of open price and at the monthly expiry of all around the open price like fools. So, if the market moves one-sidedly, it is natural that you will get nervous and all your positions will appear as a loss and you will become emotional and weak and book losses in all of them. Then you will visit my channel and abuse me in the comment box or vent your anger by giving a negative review in the review section of this book.

If you want to become an advanced option trader then you should be patient and judicious. After the market opens, you should wait for the first 15 minutes for the market to stabilize, you should then create your position only in Nifty, that too in monthly expiry.

Now, watch your position for the next 15 minutes. Now create a position in Bank Nifty in weekly expiry. After that, again watch both the positions for the next 15 minutes. Then decide whether you want to create a third position today of an open price selling straddle or not! Then, if necessary, create a third position in Fin Nifty at next week's expiry.

Now you will ask - then how will I get the premium of open price? We will be late by 45 minutes after opening!

I have already mentioned in this book that the open price premium is just for illustration. You only have to use the open price to select the strike price. Otherwise, even if you are late in making a short straddle, it will not make much difference because the premiums of call and put move opposite to each other. Therefore, when the premium in one decreases, the premium in the other increases.

Now, in the next chapter you will learn about the Share Genius Short Strangle.

❑

6

How Did the Share Genius Short Strangle Method Help Earn 12 Percent Monthly Returns?

You have to use the Share Genius Short Strangle method in monthly expiry series of Nifty and in weekly expiry series of Bank Nifty/Fin Nifty.

As per Strangle's rule, you have to select the expiry of both call and put. In this, you cannot sell call for monthly expiry and put for weekly expiry.

In a strangle, the strike price of call-put can be different, but the expiry for both must always be the same. Now let us understand how to select the strike price in Share Genius Short Strangle.

For this, have a look at the Nifty data of the previous day on which you are going to make Share Genius Short Straddle. From that data, note down the high and low prices of the previous day. For example, the October 2022 series of Nifty Option started on September 30, 2022.

On September 30, 2022, you wanted to make a Share Genius Short Strangle in the Nifty October 2022 expiry series in intraday. So, look at the Nifty data of September 29, 2022, which is a day before September 30, 2022.

Date	Opened	Highest	Lowest	Closed
September 29, 2022	16,993.6	17,026.05	16,788.6	16,818.1

That is, on September 29, Nifty reached a maximum high of 17,026.05 and a minimum low of 16,788.60. Now, here we have a simple assumption that if the Nifty trades range bound in today's trade, then it will be difficult for it to go above the previous day's high, above the previous day's high and below the previous day's low.

Therefore, the strike price that we will select to sell the call will be the strike price just above this previous day's high of 17,026.05, i.e. we will sell the call of 17,050 and the strike price that we will select for the put will be exactly below the previous day's low. Here, the previous day's low is 16,788.60, hence, we will sell the put of 16,750.

Here, you can ask two questions –

1. Is the data of the previous day of the above-mentioned Nifty of spot price or future price?
2. If the above data is of spot price then how can you use it in options because do you not know that the option market does not run on the basis of spot price but on the basis of future price?

I have mentioned these two questions because similar questions are often asked by my followers in the comments on my YouTube channel. The answer is simple –

1. The above data of Nifty is of spot price and we have to select the strike price on the basis of previous day's spot price only and not on the basis of future price.

2. I know that the options market does not work on the basis of spot price but on the basis of future price. But that is the characteristic of my methods wherein we decide future prices on the basis of spot prices. Now if we use the prices of future beforehand, then how can the future be decided on the basis of future?

Well, going into more detail now would be deviating from the main point. Let me bring you back to the point of our discussion that the strike price that we will select to sell the call is exactly above the Nifty spot price's previous high of 17,026.05. That means we will sell the call for ₹ 17,050 and select a strike price exactly below the previous day's low for the put. Here the previous day's low is 16,788.60, so we will sell the put of 16,750.

I will now provide you the complete historical data of selling calls in the series with expiry of October 27, 2022 in the following table –

Table-5

Date	Opened	Highest	Lowest	Closed	Call Sale	Premium Received	Square Off in the last 30 Minutes of Closing	Profit/Loss
29-Sep-22	16,993.6	17,026.05	16,788.6	16,818.1				
30-Sep-22	16,798.05	17,187.1	16,747.7	17,094.35	17,050	271.95	378	-5,302.5
03-Oct-22	17,102.1	17,114.65	16,855.55	16,887.35	17,200	283.6	211.95	3,582.5
04-Oct-22	17,147.45	17,287.3	17,117.3	17,274.3	17,150	300	401.25	-5,062.5
06-Oct-22	17,379.25	17,428.8	17,315.65	17,331.8	17,300	349.95	311.85	1,905
07-Oct-22	17,287.2	17,337.35	17,216.95	17,314.65	17,450	217.1	224.4	-365
10-Oct-22	17,094.35	17,280.15	17,064.7	17,241	17,350	175.1	213.55	-1,922.5
11-Oct-22	17,256.05	17,261.8	16,950.3	16,983.55	17,300	224.65	145.45	3,960
12-Oct-22	17,025.55	17,142.35	16,960.05	17,123.6	17,300	164.9	183.8	-945
13-Oct-22	17,087.35	17,112.35	16,956.95	17,014.35	17,150	225	193.4	1,580
14-Oct-22	17,322.3	17,348.55	17,169.75	17,185.7	17,150	286	247.3	1,935
17-Oct-22	17,144.8	17,328.55	17,098.55	17,311.8	17,350	144.85	180.2	-1,767.5
18-Oct-22	17,438.75	17,527.8	17,434.05	17,486.95	17,350	250	268.6	-930
19-Oct-22	17,568.15	17,607.6	17,472.85	17,512.25	17,550	154.95	132.2	1,137.5
20-Oct-22	17,423.1	17,584.15	17,421	17,563.95	17,650	82.3	86.3	-200
21-Oct-22	17,622.85	17,670.15	17,520.75	17,576.3	17,600	120	93.3	1,335
24-Oct-22	17,736.35	17,777.55	17,707.4	17,730.75	17,700	**Deepawali option market closed**		
25-Oct-22	17,808.3	17,811.5	17,637	17,656.35	17,800	80	18.95	3,052.5
27-Oct-22	17,771.4	17,783.9	17,654.5	17,736.95	**Do not take a position on expiry day**			
Total profit/Loss of the month								**1,992.5**

When you look at this table, you get an idea of how we have selected a strike price exactly above the previous day's highest to sell the call. You can also see in the above table that for the entire month (except the expiry day) we made a profit of around ₹ 1,992.50 in just the call selling leg by creating Share Genius Short Strangle in this way.

You can also see in the above table that there are two trading days in the month, September 30, 2022 and October 4, 2022, when we incurred a loss of more than ₹ 2,000 in selling calls. There was a loss of 5,302.50 on September 30, 2022. Here, if we had kept the stop loss rule at a maximum loss of ₹ 2,000 (two thousand) in one leg, then we would not have incurred an additional loss of ₹ 3,302.50.

Similarly, on October 4, 2022, too, there was a loss of ₹ 5,062.50 in the call. Here too, if we had covered the strangle with the maximum loss of ₹ 2,000, we could have made an overall profit by adding the profit from the put. I don't have historical data here. But you can understand that when the premium in call increased due to the rise in the market, it also decreased in put in the same proportion.

Therefore, the overall profit in a month, which as we can see is ₹ 1,992.50 in this leg of selling calls by keeping the stop loss, could have been much higher than this. Now in the series of October 27, 2022, by selecting the strike price according to this method (strike price one step below the lowest level of the previous day) and selling puts throughout the month, then as per the historical data, the profit of ₹ 10,747.50 made in the entire month was as follows:

Table-6

Date	Opened	Highest	Lowest	Closed	Call Sale	Premium Received	Square Off in the Last 30 Minutes of Closing	Profit/Loss
29-Sep-22	16,993.6	17,026.05	16,788.6	16,818.1				
30-Sep-22	16,798.05	17,187.1	16,747.7	17,094.35	16,750	347.05	242.45	5,230
03-Oct-22	17,102.1	17,114.65	16,855.55	16,887.35	16,700	240.05	274.65	-1,730
04-Oct-22	17,147.45	17,287.3	17,117.3	17,274.3	16,850	230	163.65	3,317.5
06-Oct-22	17,379.25	17,428.8	17,315.65	17,331.8	17,100	165.45	210.7	-2,262.5
07-Oct-22	17,287.2	17,337.35	17,216.95	17,314.65	17,300	304.95	272.05	1,645
10-Oct-22	17,094.35	17,280.15	17,064.7	17,241	17,200	318.85	261.6	2,862.5
11-Oct-22	17,256.05	17,261.8	16,950.3	16,983.55	17,050	211.65	320.1	-5,422.5
12-Oct-22	17,025.55	17,142.35	16,960.05	17,123.6	16,950	277.05	206.1	3,547.5
13-Oct-22	17,087.35	17,112.35	16,956.95	17,014.35	16,950	216.55	241.05	-1,225
14-Oct-22	17,322.3	17,348.55	17,169.75	17,185.7	16,950	113.7	132	-915
17-Oct-22	17,144.8	17,328.55	17,098.55	17,311.8	17,150	220.05	149.75	3,515
18-Oct-22	17,438.75	17,527.8	17,434.05	17,486.95	17,050	80	51.9	1,405
19-Oct-22	17,568.15	17,607.6	17,472.85	17,512.25	17,400	114.85	121.85	-350
20-Oct-22	17,423.1	17,584.15	17,421	17,563.95	17,450	156	100.4	2,780
21-Oct-22	17,622.85	17,670.15	17,520.75	17,576.3	17,400	64	53.9	505
24-Oct-22	17,736.35	17,777.55	17,707.4	17,730.75	17,500	**Deepawali option market closed**		
25-Oct-22	17,808.3	17,811.5	17,637	17,656.35	17,700	47.5	90.6	-2,155
27-Oct-22	17,771.4	17,783.9	17,654.5	17,736.95	**Do not take a position on expiry day**			
Total profit/Loss of the month								**10,747.5**

You can see in the above table that there was a loss of ₹ 2,262.50 and ₹ 5,422.50 on October 6, 2022 and October 11, 2022 respectively. Again, here also, the loss could have been limited by using the maximum stop loss of ₹ 2,000. Thus, overall, if we had made this Stock Genius Short Strangle for the entire month even without using stop loss, we would have made a profit of ₹ 1,992.50 in calls and ₹ 10,747.50 in selling puts in the entire month.

That is, the profit of call and put together would have been ₹ 1,992.50+10,747.50=12,740 in the entire month, which is around 12 percent of our margin money of ₹ 1 lakh.

Here, you can also see that if you had made use of stop loss, this profit could have gone up even more. If after reading this chapter you get overexcited and start making Share Genius Short Strangle recklessly and later start blaming or cursing me when you incur a loss, then all that will be the result of your greed and your foolhardiness.

Always remember that along with keeping the stop loss, each of my methods has a limit of shorting only 1 lot each.

Yes, you can create Share Genius Short Strangle by shorting 1 lot each of call-put in both Nifty and Bank Nifty. In trading, especially options trading, no method is 100 percent safe and effective. That's why I had mentioned the requirement of ₹ 15 lakh margin money initially so that you can try different methods simultaneously.

Sometimes it may happen that you would suffer a loss in both Share Genius Short Straddle and Share Genius Short Strangle. But you do not need to panic. More methods will be explained further in this book. Using all of them simultaneously will earn you profit overall.

❑

7

Qualities of a Successful Options Trader

You must have read my book 'How Did Abdul Go from Zero to Hero in Share Market?' The book mentions a character named Yogendra.

Recently, Yogendra's father's lungs were filled with water (in medical terms it is called 'pleurisy'). He took treatment from a doctor for 4 months. Then, when he could not find any relief, he asked for my advice.

I am also a good personal consultant to my friends. So, I advised him to consult another doctor and took him with me to the hospital of a doctor friend of mine (Dr. Purohit).

Dr. Purohit first scolded us and also the previous treating doctor about how that doctor could not diagnose that his patient's lungs were filled with water and that for 4 months he kept giving him medicines for a cold and cough.

Then Dr. Purohit said, "A doctor should have eyesight like an owl, who can immediately diagnose what the patient is suffering from." I appreciated Dr. Purohit's adivce. I can also say this as a general rule of thumb for options trading: "An options trader should be like an owl."

Please do not laugh. I mean what I am saying. Just as the owl has keen eyesight, the option trader should also keep an eye on his positions like an owl and as soon as he sees a loss above ₹ 2,000 (two thousand) in any leg, he should quickly act and cover his position.

Similarly, do not be too greedy or grasping about profits. If you are making a decent profit, then do not be too greedy. Second, owls do not have a brain. In the same way, the option trader should not try to be too smart because trying to be too clever can lead to increased losses.

In this context, I would like to refer to a follower's comment on my YouTube video. One of my followers wrote – 'Sir, good morning! Whatever I earned from straddle in the last 2 months was gone in a single day yesterday and I have now incurred a loss of ₹ 9,000. In the last one year I have lost more than ₹ 1 lakh in options trading. I gained a lot of knowledge from your videos. But the more knowledge I gained, the more money I lost. This clearly means that knowledge is responsible for losses in option trading.' I found his comment very interesting. After reading this comment, I remembered what Dr. Purohit had said. I thought this follower was saying that 'Too much knowledge is responsible for my losses in options trading. So, it makes sense that an options trader should be an owl.'

I found all this very interesting. So, I wrote to him to send me details of his trade. In response to my e-mail, I received an elaborate e-mail from him. I have added that email as it is in this book for your information. You may find it boring to read it. But read this e-mail carefully. It contains a great deal of knowledge about how a retail investor loses money in options trading.

An e-mail from one of my followers –

Sir, good morning!

Whatever I earned from straddle in 2 months was lost in a single day yesterday and now I have incurred a loss of ₹ 9,000.

Yesterday, at 10.15, when I saw the market flatten, I created a strangle. I made a strangle by selling a call of ₹ 17,600 and a put of ₹ 17,350. But when I saw huge losses in it by 1 o'clock, I created a straddle by selling a call of ₹ 17,300 and a put of ₹ 17,300 at 1 o'clock. But this time, there was an even bigger loss.

And yesterday morning, when a friend of mine saw the market going flat like me, made a straddle at 10.15 by selling a call of ₹ 17,450 and a put of ₹ 17,450. He has incurred a loss of more than ₹ 15,000. Over the last two months, I really worked hard on the straddle; I sat in front of the screen for hours. Since 4.30 am yesterday, I have been reading about how to take trades today.

I have lost count as to how many hours I worked day and night this way. But everything was in vain and futile. Now, I feel that the common man cannot earn a regular income from trading. Initially, he manages to earn a little. But one day, in a shocking development, he incurs huge losses. The same thing happened in my case in straddle. For 15-20 consecutive days, it went from 500 to 2,000. It even went from 1,000 to 2,000 3-4 times. But I was still in profit. But then there was an immense loss for 2 or 3 consecutive days. All the profit turned into a big loss.

Excuse me, sir, but today I will not stop myself from speaking up. In trading, the common man gets robbed and is ruined. Yesterday morning, the big fund houses, who were probably the operators, took the market up for an hour (while the global market was weak. I was studying since 4.30 am in the morning. I studied from all angles). After that, those rogue operators booked their profits, then kept the market flat for half an hour and then crashed it unilaterally.

Those who bought the call initially incurred losses. Then they kept the market flat and allowed us to make strangle. Then they crashed the market and ruined us, too.

Those who bought put were able to earn marginally because there was a lot of theta decay yesterday.

Sir, after 1.5 years of hard work, I am facing a loss of ₹ 1.15 lakhs in trading. I studied for many hours, watched videos, joined webinars. But everything is in vain; nothing worked.

A common man can earn only by investing in blue chip stocks for 5 to 10 years. Everything else is useless.

I am very disappointed.

Thank you, Sir.

Thank you very much.

Yours,

Anuj

(I am not mentioning his name to maintain his privacy.)

I was also confused upon reading his e-mail because the strike price that he selected or the way he made the trades was never mentioned by me in any of the videos. I had spoken neither about taking trades when the market goes flat nor about studying theta decay. Now you may read what I wrote in response to him.

In reply, I wrote to him –

Respected Sir,

Namaskar!

1. Which rule did you apply while selecting the strike prices of 17,600 and 17,350? I did not mention any such rule in any of my videos. Physics is based on certain rules. Similarly, if you take trades without following the rules, you will only incur losses. (This follower of mine runs a science coaching centre. Hence, I gave him the example of physics.)
2. Second rule: I also did not talk about taking more than one trade per day and then averaging it.
3. Third, why didn't you follow the rule of keeping a total stop loss of 2,000?

Sir, I think you are unable to control your emotions. You are also unable to set a stop loss. You approach trading more by your own discretion than by learning the rules. So, if options trading doesn't suit you, please don't try it. You should consider your blue-chip methods as correct and continue to deal in them.

Sincerely yours,

Mahesh Chandra Kaushik

My follower responded to my reply in the following manner –

Respected Mahesh Sir,

Greetings!

I agree with all your points. It is not your fault at all. I alone am responsible for my loss. I try to use my mind all the time.

Short strangle works only sideways, i.e., in a flat market and on that day (March 13, 2023) the market fell very rapidly.

That day, i.e. on March 13, 2023, the market opened at 17,164 and then it went to a high of 17,529. After that, it fell and made the lowest level of 17,113.

But the market became flat in the morning for one hour between 10 and 11. So, I made a short strangle by selling a call of ₹ 17,600 and a put of ₹ 17,350. But after 11.30 am, the market started falling. Due to this, I made profit in the call of ₹ 17,600 that I had sold. But I incurred a huge loss in the put that I had sold for ₹ 17,350. So, I made adjustments.

You did not teach how to make adjustments in straddle and strangle. But there is another market guru who teaches how to make such adjustments. As per his suggestions, I made adjustments - I squared off the call of ₹ 17,600 and sold the call of ₹ 17,500. But then after 1 hour, I also squared off the call of ₹ 17,500 and then sold the call of ₹ 17,350 and earned a small amount. As I made adjustments, my short strangle of that day became a short straddle because in the end, both the call at ₹ 17,350 and put at ₹ 17,350 were shorted.

But that day the market fell by 300 points in a day, due to which I sold put for 17,350. There was a tremendous loss in that. So, even after three adjustments, I still incurred a huge loss. The market guru who taught me adjustment himself incurred a loss of ₹ 3 lakh 75 thousand on a capital of ₹ 2 crore.

Sir, I am starting a new batch of my coaching classes from March 22. I need your blessings. From now till the month of May, I will focus only on my coaching classes. I will try to learn this again after that because new admissions to coaching classes take place till May. Also, the children taking admission in between have to be given extra classes, too.

I want to learn it no matter how much loss I may have to incur because I love studying and learning something new.

This is exciting. Just like people enjoy risking their lives in adventure sports, similarly option trading has become an adventure for me now. It has become heavily manipulated. But with risk management, one can achieve something through it. I want to learn to earn through this.

But not now. I will do something about it only after May.

I will wait for your new video.

With best wishes,

Sincerely,

Anuj

So, overall, it is proved that trying to work according to your wish only leads to more losses in options trading. Instead of making the above adjustments, if he had simply placed a stop loss on the put of ₹ 17,350 and booked a loss if the loss went above ₹ 2,000, his trade would have been highly profitable. His market guru, who had taught him adjustment, would also have followed my advice and would not take positions in more than one lot in one method. As a result, he would also not have had to incur a loss of ₹ 3,75,000 on a capital of ₹ 2 crore.

To sum it up, the option trader should be like an owl. They should keep a close eye on the profit and stop loss and works according to the methods mentioned in the strategy without applying their mind too much.

As I have often said before, trading is an art that cannot be learned by just reading books and watching videos. You will have to constantly learn and improve, and then one day you will become a successful options trader.

❑

8

The Owl Short Strangle Method

Have you read Chapter 4 of this book completely without turning the pages quickly?

I hope you have read Chapter 4 of this book thoroughly. If you have not read Chapter 4 carefully, then I will first repeat some lines from that chapter because from those very lines you will get the idea of the Owl Short Strangle Method which I am going to tell you about now.

In long straddle, call and put of the same strike price are purchased together. Long straddle is profitable only when there is an appreciable movement in one direction in the market. This type of straddle is more profitable only on the day of a big event, like on the day of the announcement of budget, day of election result, etc.

In general, there is no possibility of a big move in the market every day. Therefore, if you use Long Straddle continuously for a length time, then the chances of getting a profit from it are generally low.

For example, on March 3, 2023, Nifty opened at 17,451.25. Accordingly, if you had simultaneously bought a call-put at the nearest strike price of ₹ 17,450, it would have been a long straddle. Let us see what results you would have had if you had made this kind of long straddle in intraday on March 3, 2023! We will use open and close price data for back-test. On March 3, 2023, the call of ₹ 17,450 opened at ₹ 218.95, that is, if you had bought it as soon as the market opened, you would have bought it for around ₹ 218.95. There was a big move in the market on that day and Nifty closed at 17,594.35. That means, by the time the market closed, the call of 17,450 closed at 330.45.

So, theoretically speaking, on a call of ₹ 17,450 bought at this open price, you would have made a profit of approximately ₹ 330.45-218.95=111.50 per share and on a lot of 50 of Nifty, you would have made a profit of ₹ 5,575. Now let us look at the result of the reverse trade, in which you would have bought a put of ₹ 17,450 to create a long straddle. On March 3, 2023, its open price was 193.35 and close price was 115.90, which means that you would have incurred a loss of ₹ 77.45 per share. As it was a Nifty 50 lot, you would have lost ₹ 3,872.50 in this trade. Overall, you would have made a profit of ₹ 5,575 and incurred a loss of ₹ 3,872.50 in this long straddle and at the time of the market closing, you would have made an intraday profit of ₹ 1,702.50.

But on this day, when the market closed, it was 272.45 points (1.57 percent) higher than its previous close. Hence, you benefited from the long straddle. Long straddle in intraday is profitable only when there is a simultaneous movement of at least 1 to 1.50 percent in the market.

However, the market does not go up or rise by 1 to 1.50 percent every day through the entire month. Therefore, if you use long straddle in intraday every day through the entire month, then you will benefit only when there is a big move on 4-5 days of the month. But if there is less movement in the market, you will incur loss on that day. Overall, you will incur losses for the entire month.

Now after reading the above lines, pay close attention to the previous chapter (Chapter 7), in which I had said that a successful option trader is like an owl, who earns easily without being over smart.

So, this method is called 'Owl Short Strangle' because you do not have to use your brain for it much. There is simple, straightforward mathematics in this. This mathematics is that "Long straddle is profitable only when there is a move of 1 to 1.50 percent in the market". So, the reverse of it is that if there is no move of 1 to 1.50 percent in the market, then those who sell call-puts, i.e. those who short, will benefit.

That's it. You got the mantra of this method right here that generally a move of 1 to 1.50 percent in the market is a major move, which does not occur every day. At the most, this occurs 4-5 times during the entire month.

To understand this fact more clearly, have a look at the data of Nifty series with expiry of March 2023. This series started from February 24, 2023 and expired on March 29, 2023. You can see the data of Nifty 50 of this series in the following table –

Table-7

Date	Opened	Highest	Lowest	Closed	Opened-Closed	Movement in Percentage
24-Feb-23	17,591.35	17,599.75	17,421.8	17,465.8	-125.5	-0.71
27-Feb-23	17,428.6	17,451.6	17,299	17,392.7	-35.9	-0.21
28-Feb-23	17,383.25	17,440.45	17,255.2	17,303.95	-79.3	-0.46
01-Mar-23	17,360.1	17,467.75	17,345.25	17,450.9	90.8	0.52
02-Mar-23	17,421.5	17,445.8	17,306	17,321.9	-99.6	-0.57
03-Mar-23	17,451.25	17,644.75	17,427.7	17,594.35	143.1	0.82
06-Mar-23	17,680.35	17,799.95	17,671.95	17,711.45	31.1	0.18
08-Mar-23	17,665.75	17,766.5	17,602.25	17,754.4	88.65	0.50
09-Mar-23	17,772.05	17,772.35	17,573.6	17,589.6	-182.5	-1.03
10-Mar-23	17,443.8	17,451.5	17,324.35	17,412.9	-30.9	-0.18
13-Mar-23	17,421.9	17,529.9	17,113.45	17,154.3	-267.6	-1.54
14-Mar-23	17,160.55	17,224.65	16,987.1	17,043.3	-117.3	-0.68
15-Mar-23	17,166.45	17,211.35	16,938.9	16,972.15	-194.3	-1.13
16-Mar-23	16,994.65	17,062.45	16,850.15	16,985.6	-9.05	-0.05
17-Mar-23	17,111.8	17,145.8	16,958.15	17,100.05	-11.75	-0.07
20-Mar-23	17,066.6	17,066.6	16,828.35	16,988.4	-78.2	-0.46
21-Mar-23	17,060.4	17,127.7	17,016	17,107.5	47.1	0.28
22-Mar-23	17,177.45	17,207.25	17,107.85	17,151.9	-25.55	-0.15
23-Mar-23	17,097.4	17,205.4	17,045.3	17,076.9	-20.5	-0.12
24-Mar-23	17,076.2	17,109.45	16,917.35	16,945.05	-131.2	-0.77
27-Mar-23	16,984.3	17,091	16,918.55	16,985.7	1.4	0.01
28-Mar-23	17,031.75	17,061.75	16,913.75	16,951.7	-80.05	-0.47
29-Mar-23	16,977.3	17,126.15	16,940.6	17,080.7	103.4	0.61

In the above table, you must have noticed that in the entire series, there was a move of more than 1 percent in Nifty 50 only on 3 days, which was as follows –

Date	Move from Open in Nifty	Movement in Percentage
March 9, 2023	-182.45	-1.03
March 13, 2023	-267.60	-1.54
March 15, 2023	-194.30	-1.13

It is worth noting here that this move is from the open price of Nifty. This move is not from the previous day's close price. If you sell options on the basis of open price, then most of the part of the potential rise or fall based on sentiment in the market on that day is already discounted due to the opening of gap-up or gap-down market.

You can see in this table how much gap-up or gap-down Nifty opened in the entire month in the series of March 2023 –

Table-8

Date	Opened	Highest	Lowest	Closed	Closed- Opened	Movement in Percentage	Gap up or Gap down
24-Feb-23	17,591.35	17,599.75	17,421.8	17,465.8	-125.55	-0.71	
27-Feb-23	17,428.6	17,451.6	17,299	17,392.7	-35.9	-0.21	-37.2
28-Feb-23	17,383.25	17,440.45	17,255.2	17,303.95	-79.3	-0.46	-9.45
01-Mar-23	17,360.1	17,467.75	17,345.25	17,450.9	90.8	0.52	56.15
02-Mar-23	17,421.5	17,445.8	17,306	17,321.9	-99.6	-0.57	-29.4
03-Mar-23	17,451.25	17,644.75	17,427.7	17,594.35	143.1	0.82	129.35
06-Mar-23	17,680.35	17,799.95	17,671.95	17,711.45	31.1	0.18	86
08-Mar-23	17,665.75	17,766.5	17,602.25	17,754.4	88.65	0.50	-45.7
09-Mar-23	17,772.05	17,772.35	17,573.6	17,589.6	-182.45	-1.03	17.65
10-Mar-23	17,443.8	17,451.5	17,324.35	17,412.9	-30.9	-0.18	-145.8
13-Mar-23	17,421.9	17,529.9	17,113.45	17,154.3	-267.6	-1.54	9
14-Mar-23	17,160.55	17,224.65	16,987.1	17,043.3	-117.25	-0.68	6.25
15-Mar-23	17,166.45	17,211.35	16,938.9	16,972.15	-194.3	-1.13	123.15
16-Mar-23	16,994.65	17,062.45	16,850.15	16,985.6	-9.05	-0.05	22.5
17-Mar-23	17,111.8	17,145.8	16,958.15	17,100.05	-11.75	-0.07	126.2
20-Mar-23	17,066.6	17,066.6	16,828.35	16,988.4	-78.2	-0.46	-33.45
21-Mar-23	17,060.4	17,127.7	17,016	17,107.5	47.1	0.28	72
22-Mar-23	17,177.45	17,207.25	17,107.85	17,151.9	-25.55	-0.15	69.95
23-Mar-23	17,097.4	17,205.4	17,045.3	17,076.9	-20.5	-0.12	-54.5
24-Mar-23	17,076.2	17,109.45	16,917.35	16,945.05	-131.15	-0.77	-0.7
27-Mar-23	16,984.3	17,091	16,918.55	16,985.7	1.4	0.01	39.25
28-Mar-23	17,031.75	17,061.75	16,913.75	16,951.7	-80.05	-0.47	46.05
29-Mar-23	16,977.3	17,126.15	16,940.6	17,080.7	103.4	0.61	25.6

Therefore, the simple mathematics in this Owl Short Strangle is that after the market opens, you should look at the open price of the market.

Or when you want to make an owl short strangle, you should look at the current market price of Nifty 50 of that particular time.

Most of the boom or recession in this current market price will have already been discounted due to the gap-up or gap-down opening.

Now considering a maximum of 1.50 percent bullishness or recession as possible, calculate the level of 1.50 percent above and 1.50 percent below the current market price.

For example, the open price of Nifty on February 24, 2023 was 17,591.35. The1.50 percent level above it was 17,855.22. Now, look at the strike price of its nearest call. Naturally, out of 17,850 and 17,900, the nearest call of 17,855.22 is the strike price of 17,850. So, you have to sell the call of 17,850 in the Owl Strangle Method.

Similarly, after deducting 1.50 percent from 17,591.35, the result we get is 17,327.48. Its nearest strike price will be 17,350. We have to take the nearest strike, whether it is below or above 17,327.48.

Here, out of 17,300 and 17,350, the strike of 17,350 is closer to 17,327.48. That is why we have selected that. Had it been 17,323, we would have selected 17,300. So, now we will also sell the put of ₹ 17,350.

That is, in the Owl Strangle Method, whenever you take a trade after the market opens and the gap-up or gap-down opening has been properly adjusted, you have to sell the call at about 1.50 percent above and the put at about 1.50 percent below of that time.

Remember here that in the book, to help you understand, call has been sold at about 1.50 percent above the open price and put at about 1.50 percent below the open price.

But, in practice, whenever you make an Owl Short Strangle in the first 30 minutes of trading after the market is open, take the price (which is usually around the open price) of that time and sell a call about 1.50 percent above it and a put about 1.50 percent below it.

Now on February 24, 2023, the result of this owl strangle method was as follows –

Call/Put	Open Price Premium	Close Price Premium	Intraday Profit/ Loss on Short
17,800 Call	198.00	134.30	3,185.00
17,350 Put	148.20	167.20	-950.00
Overall Profit = 2235			

Now, if you had sold only calls for the entire month for the expiry of March 29, 2023 using the Owl Strangle method (around the open price in intraday) and covered in the last 30 minutes of intraday, then according to the following table, you would have made a profit of approximately ₹ 16,927.50 in the whole month –

Table-9

Date	Opened	Closed	1.5 percent more than opening	Call Sale	Premium Received	Closed on Premium	Profit-Loss in One Lot
24-Feb-23	17,591.35	17,465.8	17,855.22	17,850	170	115.45	2,727.50
27-Feb-23	17,428.6	17,392.7	17,690.03	17,700	160.05	139.3	1,037.50
28-Feb-23	17,383.25	17,303.95	17,644.00	17,650	160	119.95	2,002.50
01-Mar-23	17,360.1	17,450.9	17,620.50	17,600	150	178.35	-1,417.50
02-Mar-23	17,421.5	17,321.9	17,682.82	17,700	134.75	84.75	2,500.00
03-Mar-23	17,451.25	17,594.35	17,713.02	17,700	95.4	176.45	-4,052.50
06-Mar-23	17,680.35	17,711.45	17,945.56	17,950	89.95	104.65	-735.00
08-Mar-23	17,665.75	17,754.4	17,930.74	17,950	78.5	110.15	-1,582.50
09-Mar-23	17,772.05	17,589.6	18,038.63	18,050	163.9	97.9	3,300.00
10-Mar-23	17,443.8	17,412.9	17,705.46	17,700	107.5	80.15	1,367.50
13-Mar-23	17,421.9	17,154.3	17,683.23	17,700	86.55	48.95	1,880.00
14-Mar-23	17,160.55	17,043.3	17,417.96	17,400	130.25	96.05	1,710.00
15-Mar-23	17,166.45	16,972.15	17,423.95	17,400	120	64.9	2,755.00
16-Mar-23	16994.65	16,985.6	17,249.57	17,250	106.7	108.45	-87.50
17-Mar-23	17,111.8	17,100.05	17,368.48	17,350	100	89.45	527.50
20-Mar-23	17,066.6	16,988.4	17,322.60	17,300	99	61.5	1,875.00
21-Mar-23	17,060.4	17,107.5	17,316.31	17,300	69.15	82.8	-682.50
22-Mar-23	17,177.45	17,151.9	17,435.11	17,450	45	37.45	377.50
23-Mar-23	17,097.4	17,076.9	17,353.86	17,350	70	26.65	2,167.50
24-Mar-23	17,076.2	16,945.05	17,332.34	17,350	23.2	8.8	720.00
27-Mar-23	16,984.3	16,985.7	17,239.06	17,250	18.75	11.4	367.50
28-Mar-23	17,031.75	16,951.7	17,287.23	17,300	5	1.6	170.00
29-Mar-23	16,977.3	17,080.7	17,231.96	17,250	**No Trade on Expiry Day**		0.00
						Total	**16,927.50**

Now, on the contrary, if you had also sold the put, you would have incurred a loss of ₹ 6,130 in the entire month as per the following table –

Table-10

Date	Opened	Closed	1.5 percent more than opening	Put Sale	Premium Received	Closed on Premium	Profit-Loss in One Lot
24-Feb-23	17,591.35	17,465.8	17,327.48	17,350	148.2	167.2	-950
27-Feb-23	17,428.6	17,392.7	17,167.17	17,150	149.7	119.9	1,490
28-Feb-23	17,383.25	17,303.95	17,122.50	17,150	119.95	143.25	-1,165
01-Mar-23	17,360.1	17,450.9	17,099.70	17,100	118	82.4	1,780
02-Mar-23	17,421.5	17,321.9	17,160.18	17,150	95.55	126.8	-1,562.5
03-Mar-23	17,451.25	17,594.35	17,189.48	17,200	115	62.95	2,602.5
06-Mar-23	17,680.35	17,711.45	17,415.14	17,400	85.05	71.85	660
08-Mar-23	17,665.75	17,754.4	17,400.76	17,400	75.2	70.45	237.5
09-Mar-23	17,772.05	17,589.6	17,505.47	17,500	85.5	132.55	-2352.5
10-Mar-23	17,443.8	17,412.9	17,182.14	17,200	93	103.85	-542.5
13-Mar-23	17,421.9	17,154.3	17,160.57	17,150	94.95	204.95	-5500
14-Mar-23	17,160.55	17,043.3	16,903.14	16,900	125	136.05	-552.5
15-Mar-23	17,166.45	16,972.15	16,908.95	16,900	91	159.85	-3,442.5
16-Mar-23	16,994.65	16,985.6	16,739.73	16,750	124.15	107.45	835
17-Mar-23	17,111.8	17,100.05	16,855.12	16,850	95	69.5	1,275
20-Mar-23	17,066.6	16,988.4	16,810.60	16,800	79.6	95.2	-780
21-Mar-23	17,060.4	17,107.5	16,804.49	16,800	79.8	47.4	1,620
22-Mar-23	17,177.45	17,151.9	16,919.79	16,900	52.1	50.85	62.5
23-Mar-23	17,097.4	17,076.9	16,840.94	16,850	47.95	42.3	282.5
24-Mar-23	17,076.2	16,945.05	16,820.06	16,800	30	55.6	-1,280
27-Mar-23	16,984.3	16,985.7	16,729.54	16,750	35	15.1	995
28-Mar-23	17,031.75	16,951.7	16,776.27	16,800	13.8	10.65	157.5
29-Mar-23	16,977.3	17,080.7	16,722.64	16,700			0
						Total	**-6,130**

So, overall, you would have made an overall profit of ₹ 10,797 and 50 paise in the entire month (i.e. after deducting the loss of ₹ 6,130 from the profit of ₹ 16,927.50, the balance remaining is ₹ 10,797.50).

Now, here it is also worth noting the fact that in the above example, I have not taken into account the stop loss of ₹ 2,000, whereas there is also a rule that whether in case of call or put, if there is a loss of above ₹ 2,000, you should cover it and you should cover the profitable position around the time of market close.

If we had done the same in the above table in the trade dated March 3, 2023, the loss in the call on that day would have been limited to ₹ 2,000 instead of -4,052.50 and if you had made profit in 2,602.50 put that day, you would have made an overall profit of 2,602.50-2,000=602.50, whereas in the above example, we have considered the total loss on that day to be -4,052.50 and overall loss to be -1,450.

Similarly, the loss of -5,500 incurred in the put selling leg of the trade dated March 13, 2023, could also have been limited to ₹ 2,000 with a stop loss. Therefore, in this case, too, you have to follow both the rules mentioned in the book-

1. The position should be limited to selling 1 call and put each of Nifty and Bank Nifty. If you have more margin money then you have to use other methods mentioned in the book simultaneously.
2. If you start seeing a loss of more than ₹ 2,000 (for the lot of 1 each) in any leg, then you should book loss in it and let the profitable leg continue till the market closes.

Now, some readers may have a doubt that if the profitable leg also suffers loss due to market fluctuations later on, then they will incur loss in both. But this does not happen in 90 percent of the days because the loss of above ₹ 2,000 in 1 leg shows that the market has taken a one-sided direction, which reverses only in 10 percent of the days when the market is highly volatile, otherwise it does not happen.

❑

9

Do Not Change Methods Frequently in Options Trading

As mentioned in earlier chapters, there is a higher chance of incurring losses rather than making profits if one tries to be too clever or too smart while trying to earn money in options trading.

If you have come thus far after carefully reading the earlier chapters in the book, then you must have understood that no method is 100 percent effective in options trading. Regarding all my straddle or strangle methods that you have read in the past, you must have seen that these methods give overall profit on most days of the trading month; however, sometimes, there are also losses in these methods on say 3 to 5 days.

Now, sometimes, when one incurs a loss for 3 consecutive days, it is natural that they would get fed up or exhausted with these methods. They will think that either the method itself is wrong or it needs further improvement.

Due to this, the person makes adjustments in that method in his mind. On account of this, when he would have made a profit on the next trading day using the original method, he ends up incurring a loss due to the adjustments that he made to the method.

Therefore, if you use any one method, and if you make overall profit in that method after adjusting the losses incurred in 3 to 4 trading sessions in a month, then avoid changing the methods repeatedly or avoid making unnecessary adjustments.

In this regard, the story of a kachori seller is very exciting and inspiring. Let me tell you the story of that kachori seller.

A kachori seller named Govind Bhai was very famous. He used to make special kachoris. The size of his kachori was two times bigger than the normal kachori. The kachori was filled with a very delicious filling which was prepared using various digestive items like asafoetida, lentils, peas, peanuts, cashew nuts, raisins, paneer, fenugreek, onion, potato, etc.

His kachori cost ₹ 15 each. But it was so delectable, nutritious and easily digestible that whenever he came to the market with his lorry, all his kachoris would be sold within 2 hours.

Some readers' mouths might have started watering just by reading the specialties of the kachori. It had been 12 years since he had started selling kachoris. His sales were doing very well and he was satisfied with his business and profits.

Gradually, some smart and self-declared economists from among his customers became his friends. Those friends advised him, 'Look, you make very good kachoris, you earn very well, and you also have a monopoly in the market. If you just follow some of our financial advice, you will grow phenomenally.

With our advice, your kachori lorry will turn into a kachori startup and you will start making sales worth crores.'

The kachori seller said, 'All right. What do I need to do to make sales worth crores of rupees and establish the Kachoriwala Pvt. Ltd. startup?'

Those economist friends advised him, 'All right. First, you just need to make one change. You must take advantage of your monopoly and increase the price of kachori from ₹ 15 to ₹ 25. He followed the advice. Now, some customers became upset at the price rise and his sales dropped by about 20 percent.

Those economist friends said, 'Look, this is exciting. Since the sales reduced by 20 percent, you will have to fry 20 percent less kachoris. This will save you hard work as well as material. But we have increased the price from ₹ 15 to ₹ 25, which has increased your income by 66 percent. Now even if sales have decreased by 20 percent, overall, you are earning 33 percent more income.'

The kachori seller was very happy. He asked, 'What is the next improvement that I should make?'

His friends asked whether people eat kachoris for breakfast or for dinner and lunch to have a filling meal.

The kachori seller said, 'It is simple. They eat it for breakfast.'

His friends then asked, 'Then why do you make your kachori the size of a pizza? Halve its size and make it equal to a normal kachori. This will reduce the cost by 50 percent.'

'Now what is the point of putting potatoes and peas in kachoris? They have a place in samosas. If you remove potatoes and peas from the filling, the cost will come down even further. And is it kachori or a pizza? Why do you add paneer to it? You should remove paneer as well. You should also stop adding dry fruits like cashews, raisins, etc. You are not selling kachoris to royalty! After all, only poor people on the streets eat it.

The kachori seller accepted all the suggestions because he wanted to become a millionaire quickly. Now his sales dropped further and remained only 20 percent because people realized that his kachoris had not only become expensive but its quality also had become poor.

Now his friends said, 'Don't worry, if sales have decreased by 80 percent, then the cost has also reduced. Now, we have one last suggestion for you. You should give up this dilapidated lorry and rent a place which will look like a decent restaurant. That will give the look of a startup. The lorry has a look of poverty. It will be a big restaurant like place, with attractive tables. You can hire a smart receptionist and waiters in uniforms. Then all the rich people will come to your restaurant to eat kachoris. You can then charge them ₹ 50 per kachori.'

You can guess what must have happened when the kachori seller accepted the last suggestion. Firstly, his lorry had settled there for 12 years. Secondly, it was on a busy road near two government schools in the city and passers-by and students used to have breakfast there. He lost all those customers when the lorry was removed from the spot and a restaurant-like breakfast point came into existence.

Secondly, the rich people for whom he had opened the restaurant-like breakfast point, already avoided eating fried food as they suffered from obesity, diabetes and high blood pressure. They ate boiled momos.

In a nutshell, Govind Bhai's business came to a standstill. He incurred enormous debts and lost everything. Fortunately, he was introduced to me. I advised him to again adopt the same method which he had followed for 12 years, which had made him rich and that he should park the same lorry at the same place. I told him that he should keep the price of kachoris at ₹ 15 as before and that he should revert to the old size of kachori and continue adding cashews, raisins, paneer, peas, potatoes – everything that he was adding for the last 12 years.

After he followed my advice, his business was back to normal within a month.

The gist of the story is that if, through option trading, overall, you are making profits throughout the month, or I would say that even if you incur occasional losses during the month, then you should calculate your returns for the entire year. If you get 15-20-25 percent return on capital throughout the year, then do not be greedy and do not change the methods repeatedly. Do not use new ideas for them on your own like those economist friends.

Don't be afraid of the occasional loss. Make sure to cover at less losses by using their stop losses smartly.

I would like to conclude this chapter by mentioning the famous financial writer Robert T. Kiyosaki.

Famous financial author Robert T. Kiyosaki writes in his book *'Rich Dad, Poor Dad'* that rich dad believed in the KISS principle. Here KISS means Keep It Simple or Stupid, that is, more money can be made with simple or stupid strategies.

All told, the Owl strategy is also as simple and stupid as Robert T. Kiyosaki's KISS strategy.

In the following chapters, some more strategies will also be suggested for making money in options trading using the principles of the Owl Strategy.

10

Can One Get More Reliable Data Than NSE?

I use NSE data to back-test my methods.

My followers ask in the comments as to why I don't back-test the strategies for options trading using such and such (xyz) website.

I will not name any third-party website or software. But there are many softwares and websites available in the market that claim to show such back-tests and claim to test strategies.

In fact, these are all paid service providers, which charge you monthly or yearly subscription fees for providing you with these services. When all types of data are available for free on NSE website, then why should I use the services of paid service providers just for back-testing?

I myself am a SEBI registered research analyst. My YouTube channel has more than 2 lakh followers and this number of followers can tempt anyone to exploit them to earn money.

Regarding most of the third-party service providers who are suggested to me in the comments for using their platform, I already receive e-mails from them asking me to encourage my followers to use their software/website/app for back-test and in return they will give me a hefty referral commission.

However, I stand by my principle that if I want to earn money, then I will feel proud to earn it from the share market. But I will not recommend third party software/website/app to my followers and exploit them for money.

In fact, many YouTubers give you links to these software vendors' websites/apps and ask you to back-test the options trading strategies from them so that they can earn a massive referral commission. When you repeatedly watch the videos of these YouTubers, you get fully convinced that if you want to do option trading, then first you have to get your strategies back-tested by taking a monthly subscription from them. Then they will tell you that they can give you better strategies than the strategies that you are using now. Then they will also charge separately for that. Finally, when you lose money even after using their strategies, they will tell you about stop loss, how risky the options market is, and that you should have read the disclaimer and disclosure.

All told, can any data be more reliable than the NSE data that we use for back-testing? If you really have a strong desire to do the real time back-test, I also have an idea to do the real time back-test for free.

You must have heard about paper trading! If you haven't heard about it, I will teach you. Pick up a pen and paper and half an hour after the market opens in the morning, look at the option chain and note down on paper 1-1 call panic trade (of 1-1 lot) using my methods.

Review it every 15 minutes with the market price. If there is a loss of more than ₹ 2,000 in any leg, then make a note that your stop loss has been triggered there and let the second leg run till the last half hour before the market closes.

Whatever position you have in the last half hour, note down on paper how much profit you would have made and loss you would have incurred by covering that position.

If you incur an overall loss in paper trading on the first day, it does not mean that you should consider the methods mentioned in the book as useless or worthless and discard the book.

In fact, it is just a coincidence that you started paper trading during those 4-5 trading days of the month which are loss making.

I would advise you to continue these paper trades for the whole month and only then reach a decision.

Now some readers may again pose a question, "But sir, in the back-test that you do from the historical data of NSE, it is not possible to sell either at open price or at close price. Suppose, I took a position at 9.50 in the morning and cut it at 2.50 in the afternoon, then how will I know what my purchase price at 9.50 was from the open price? And how will my cover cut value be determined from the close price after cutting the position at ₹ 2.50?

There are two answers to this question. I have already given the first answer in Chapter 4 of this book. But let me tell you once again. When you use it in practice, you will see that you can neither sell at the exact open price, nor at the exact close price. There will definitely be some difference between them. But by checking this method on the basis of open-close prices from historical data, you can make a rough estimate of your performance.

Accordingly, if on December 30, 2022, you had sold a call-put of ₹ 18,250 simultaneously based on the market's open price of ₹ 18,259.10, you would have received a premium of approximately ₹ 306.10 on the call of ₹ 18,250. Actually, on March 30, 2022, the call of 18,250 opened at 306.10. I suppose it is true that you couldn't hold it on 306.10. But it is possible that you could have earned a premium above ₹ 306.10 in the first half hour, and could have earned slightly less than that.

Overall, this would not make much difference to our calculations because if you had earned a premium of less than ₹ 306.10 on a call, you would have earned a higher premium of almost the same amount on a put. You already know that when shorting a call-put, their premiums move opposite to each other and because only if the market had fallen after opening, you would have earned less premium on your call. But in case of the market falling, the premium you would have earn on the put would have increased. Therefore, the back-test we propose to conduct with the open and close prices of call-put based on historical data will have almost the same results as a real-time practical back-test.

The second answer is that paper trading is the best and free option for this. After reading the book, you should gain experience by paper trading for at least a month and get into real trading after that.

Doing paper trade for one month is the best real time back-test. By reviewing every 15 minutes with its help, you will also get a reasonable idea of the stop loss.

But in today's world of ChatGPT and AI (Artificial Intelligence), we do not want to work hard. We waste our time by watching senseless statuses, reels, videos on our mobile and try to get ready-made data for back-test etc. from somewhere so that we can save ourselves the hard work of paper trade.

There is an employee named Moolchandji in my office. He approached me and said, 'Sir, teach me also how to earn money from the stock market.' I said to him, 'Sure. I have written 6 books about stock market. My publisher 'Prabhat Prakashan, Delhi' sends me author's copies. I will give you 6 books free of cost tomorrow and you can read them. From them, you will learn everything that I know.'

He said, 'Sir, please do not give me books because I do not have time to read books.' Now, just think how much time it must have taken for me to write 6 books, whereas readers do not even have the time to read them!

Secondly, if one could understand the stock market in a 15-minute meeting and a 5-minute phone call, then why would I write 6 books? (You are holding my seventh book.)

Overall, if you are also living a life by spending your time watching useless statuses, reels, videos, matches, etc. then this book on option trading will be of no use to you. Now, you will have to search for another book that will teach you easy methods, which will prove to be an endless search lasting a lifetime.

But if you yourself practise through paper trading, you will gradually become an expert in option trading for free.

God also helps those who help themselves. Therefore, do not avoid the hard work of paper trade. Try each method on paper trading for one month each, and after that get into real trading.

❑

11

What is the Iron Condor Strategy?

When you read the names of options trading techniques, you will feel like you have entered a zoo. In my book, you have already read about the owl strategy. Apart from this, there is also a butterfly strategy in options trading.

The strategy that you will read about in this chapter is called the Condor Strategy. The Condor a species of 'vulture'.

Condors are very large birds. These birds of the vulture class appear larger than humans. Their weight is about 15 kg and their wingspan measures up to 11 feet.

The Condors are usually found around the Andes Mountain range in Latin America. Since option trading was first started in America and because the graph of this strategy looks like a flying condor bird, this strategy was named 'Iron Condor Strategy'.

This method has been created by removing the shortcomings of short strangle. I say in a lighter vein that just as the vulture can be considered the elder brother of the owl, the Iron Condor can be considered the elder brother of the Owl Strangle.

Iron Condor is a slightly complex strategy and is difficult to understand. But I will explain it to you in a very simple manner.

To understand this strategy, it is important for you to first understand the short strangle. So, if you read this book opening random chapters, then you need to first go back to Chapters 5, 6 and 8 and understand the short strangle thoroughly from them. Only then will you be able to understand this method very well.

Briefly, the Iron Condor strategy has four parts—

1. You sell an out of the money call.
2. You buy an out of the money call at a premium lower than the premium of the sold call.
3. You sell an out of the money put. You have already understood both the above parts in the form of short strangle. Now, to limit the risk in the short strangle created in this way, you also buy 1 call-put each, i.e.
4. You buy an out of the money put at a premium that is lower than the premium of the sold put.

Do not worry if you do not understand anything. I thought this strategy was complicated. That is why I tried to explain it to you by giving practical examples along with pictures so that you could understand it very well.

You may see the option chain data of the monthly expiry of Nifty around 12.30 pm on June 1, 2023 –

CALLS											PUTS									
OI	CHNG IN OI	VOLUME	IV	LTP	CHNG	BID QTY	BID	ASK	ASK QTY	STRIKE	BID QTY	BID	ASK	ASK QTY	CHNG	LTP	IV	VOLUME	CHNG IN OI	OI
1,798	11	90	-	756.75	-11.90	50	753.75	756.10	50	17,900.00	700	36.10	36.25	800	-2.55	36.10	13.05	9,265	1,111	20,347
613	4	14	-	715.00	-9.65	200	704.65	713.85	50	17,950.00	1,250	41.00	41.20	150	-2.75	41.20	12.94	2,094	116	2,532
26,585	176	1,342	-	666.40	-10.30	50	666.55	668.40	200	18,000.00	50	47.45	47.60	1,200	-2.80	47.60	12.89	20,677	-625	99,766
190	13	23	-	609.60	-30.55	3,700	612.90	625.90	200	18,050.00	2,900	52.40	52.65	800	-2.00	53.05	12.65	1,208	-100	2,003
4,725	269	581	-	571.60	-18.55	100	578.20	579.75	200	18,100.00	850	58.75	59.00	1,050	-2.75	59.05	12.50	8,306	161	19,361
468	3	14	5.38	549.95	1.30	50	532.85	540.80	150	18,150.00	1,300	66.70	67.00	1,400	-3.20	66.65	12.40	1,245	60	1,728
13,294	870	4,186	-	497.20	-13.40	50	496.00	497.50	500	18,200.00	950	75.45	75.70	1,100	-3.00	75.60	12.28	19,348	552	57,616
1,631	-111	1,091	5.40	454.30	-8.40	450	453.50	456.10	100	18,250.00	650	84.35	84.60	150	-2.70	84.35	12.14	3,557	171	3,503
20,853	-2,146	11,478	6.55	417.00	-11.55	50	416.85	417.50	250	18,300.00	50	94.85	95.05	700	-2.35	95.00	12.01	26,987	-2,009	48,865
1,834	9	197	6.06	379.05	-11.00	100	377.60	379.20	400	18,350.00	650	106.65	107.10	1,650	-1.20	107.00	11.95	1,700	139	3,268
17,935	-2,345	11,784	7.23	342.30	-10.30	150	342.30	342.95	500	18,400.00	100	120.90	121.20	100	-2.40	120.95	11.85	22,262	-2,516	30,106
2,176	606	1,614	7.44	309.40	-8.30	300	307.50	308.35	300	18,450.00	150	135.10	135.65	150	-0.85	135.15	11.77	1,400	115	2,339
37,774	-934	35,726	7.57	274.50	-7.75	100	274.50	274.95	350	18,500.00	1,000	151.60	151.95	50	-1.85	151.65	11.66	44,879	-1,135	34,061
3,173	905	4,987	7.70	243.10	-10.45	600	243.10	243.80	450	18,550.00	100	170.20	170.70	100	-2.30	170.15	11.64	6,594	1,119	2,872
28,956	3,637	38,889	7.72	212.75	-8.90	350	212.70	213.15	50	18,600.00	50	190.05	190.40	1,300	-0.70	190.40	11.56	43,154	2,938	23,509
3,427	690	4,671	7.79	185.35	-9.05	200	185.35	185.90	100	18,650.00	50	211.65	212.20	450	-0.90	211.95	11.57	4,101	-493	1,941
22,460	608	19,287	7.79	159.90	-8.45	100	159.65	159.90	50	18,700.00	100	236.00	236.35	50	0.15	236.00	11.55	11,025	-884	11,250
2,739	4	2,048	7.79	137.10	-7.65	50	136.40	136.85	100	18,750.00	900	261.85	262.70	300	7.50	265.30	11.56	494	-16	347
27,708	-107	16,387	7.78	115.50	-7.10	250	115.30	115.60	800	18,800.00	50	290.05	290.50	50	-0.30	290.50	11.57	4,129	45	7,392
3,012	111	2,546	7.76	97.35	-7.95	1,050	96.55	96.95	750	18,850.00	250	320.95	321.95	250	-0.60	321.80	11.71	123	1	226
21,916	271	12,005	7.75	79.80	-6.45	200	79.70	79.90	200	18,900.00	200	353.80	354.75	300	3.95	354.25	11.82	1,501	-6	2,585
2,643	373	1,890	7.74	65.80	-5.85	200	65.40	65.60	200	18,950.00	50	387.55	393.00	150	7.90	397.20	12.38	5	-	186
77,286	894	27,250	7.81	54.60	-5.00	300	54.45	54.60	900	19,000.00	150	427.85	429.30	250	0.80	428.35	12.26	3,193	-3	23,485

Now, in this, the spot price of Nifty is 18,546.75, that is, there is an out of the money call of 18,600. So, if you had sold 1 call of 18,600 to create an Iron Condor, it would have been sold for $212.70 as per the above data.

Here you must have also noticed that instead of ask price 213.15, I have opted for bid price 212.70 because ask price is the price of a seller like you, whereas bid price is the price at which someone wants to buy. Therefore, if you had sold at the market price, you would have earned the rate of only ₹ 212.70.

Now to limit the risk in this, we will buy an out of the money call of the next level from 18,600, i.e. 18,650 at 185.90. Here, I have taken the ask price because the seller is not prepared to sell to us at a lower price than this. So, out of the four points which I had explained to you above, the first and second points are completed –

1. We sell an out of the money call.
2. We buy an out of the money call at a premium lower than the premium of the sold call.

Now the put of 18,550 is add the money put, that is, a little profit is made on 18,550 as per the market price of 18,546.75. Therefore, it cannot be considered a completely out of the money put. So, we sell an out of the money put of ₹ 18,500 at ₹ 151.60.

To cover the risk of further fall, we buy an out of the money put at the next level of 18,450 at 135.65.

Now out of the four points mentioned above, the third and fourth points have also been completed –

1. We sell an out of the money put. You have already understood both the above parts in the form of short strangle. Now, to limit the risk in the short strangle created in this way, we

also buy 1 call-put each, i.e.

2. We buy an out of the money put at a premium that is lower than the premium of the sold put.

Creating this type of iron condor is very popular among small investors and retail traders because it significantly reduces risk when you sell a call-put while also simultaneously buying the immediate next level of call-put. Therefore, the margin is also very low i.e., it is between ₹ 35,000 to ₹ 50,000.

Now see the situation around 3.15 around the time of market closure in the following picture –

CALLS											PUTS									
OI	CHNG IN OI	VOLUME	IV	LTP	CHNG	BID QTY	BID	ASK	ASK QTY	STRIKE	BID QTY	BID	ASK	ASK QTY	CHNG	LTP	IV	VOLUME	CHNG IN OI	OI
1,796	9	143	-	705.50	-63.15	400	705.45	708.65	50	17,900.00	100	42.20	42.35	50	3.60	42.25	12.83	18,050	1,263	20,499
614	5	16	-	658.00	-66.65	50	658.50	665.00	50	17,950.00	100	48.00	48.35	2,250	4.60	48.55	12.73	3,249	284	2,700
26,505	96	2,930	-	619.00	-57.70	300	620.90	622.75	100	18,000.00	50	55.80	56.00	3,950	5.55	55.95	12.73	39,419	474	1,00,865
201	24	48	10.92	561.85	-78.30	50	573.00	581.20	50	18,050.00	800	61.55	61.85	1,250	7.10	62.15	12.51	2,310	55	2,158
4,682	226	951	6.93	534.10	-56.05	150	533.40	535.00	450	18,100.00	200	69.15	69.45	100	7.40	69.20	12.36	14,642	-344	18,856
468	3	21	9.32	501.00	-47.65	50	490.85	498.25	50	18,150.00	50	77.95	78.30	1,350	9.05	78.90	12.24	2,517	246	1,914
13,256	832	7,192	8.21	455.45	-55.15	500	455.60	456.90	300	18,200.00	100	88.15	88.40	150	9.85	88.45	12.14	35,431	1,123	58,187
1,568	-174	1,284	8.22	406.80	-55.90	550	416.10	416.40	250	18,250.00	150	98.55	98.95	1,350	11.95	99.00	11.98	6,493	568	3,900
21,139	-1,860	14,862	8.40	376.05	-52.50	1,100	378.00	379.10	100	18,300.00	100	110.30	110.50	200	13.20	110.55	11.88	47,092	-312	50,562
1,761	-64	484	8.47	341.85	-48.20	600	342.05	342.65	250	18,350.00	1,350	123.30	123.45	250	15.25	123.45	11.74	3,713	-78	3,051
17,849	-2,431	20,482	8.53	308.10	-44.50	1,950	307.95	308.55	650	18,400.00	50	139.15	139.35	1,100	15.60	138.95	11.65	40,897	-3,750	28,872
2,726	1,156	3,234	8.49	274.50	-43.20	700	274.65	275.50	550	18,450.00	1,350	154.70	155.30	50	19.55	155.55	11.56	2,885	-42	2,182
39,234	526	61,302	8.49	243.00	-39.25	100	242.80	243.00	100	18,500.00	100	173.05	173.35	50	19.50	173.00	11.47	81,719	243	35,439
3,123	855	8,282	8.49	213.50	-40.05	800	213.15	213.75	1,200	18,550.00	900	192.95	193.55	50	21.05	193.50	11.41	10,624	1,105	2,858
32,740	7,421	65,488	8.44	184.20	-37.45	50	183.95	184.25	50	18,600.00	750	215.45	215.60	50	24.30	215.40	11.34	71,013	3,209	23,780
3,833	1,096	7,779	8.44	159.75	-34.65	400	159.50	159.80	50	18,650.00	700	238.55	239.20	850	27.95	240.80	11.35	6,343	-249	2,185
22,941	1,089	33,083	8.39	136.00	-32.35	50	135.90	136.20	500	18,700.00	50	264.90	265.50	700	29.60	265.45	11.34	18,119	-1,738	10,396
2,759	24	4,177	8.39	115.45	-29.30	100	115.45	115.75	1,200	18,750.00	700	294.70	295.55	600	39.15	296.95	11.39	949	69	432
31,376	3,561	37,958	8.36	97.00	-25.60	150	96.90	97.15	100	18,800.00	550	325.35	325.90	1,000	34.85	325.65	11.45	8,205	725	8,072
3,240	339	5,232	8.31	79.95	-25.35	200	79.70	79.95	50	18,850.00	500	357.35	358.35	500	44.00	366.40	11.59	361	23	248
21,901	256	28,969	8.29	65.70	-20.55	200	65.65	65.90	1,750	18,900.00	400	392.40	393.50	150	44.70	395.00	11.68	2,422	-138	2,453
3,199	929	4,398	8.23	52.70	-18.95	550	53.00	53.30	400	18,950.00	50	429.30	430.90	450	50.30	439.60	11.69	99	34	220
77,332	940	52,136	8.29	43.60	-16.00	100	43.70	43.80	1,750	19,000.00	50	470.00	471.25	450	43.65	471.20	12.17	6,208	-167	23,321

Now the market had fallen by 49.25 points to 18,485.15. The ₹ 18,600 call which was sold at ₹ 212.70 could have been covered by buying it at ₹ 184.25. In this trade, on a lot of 50, we would have made a profit of ₹ 212.70-184.25=28.45×50=1,422.50.

Now if we had sold the call of ₹ 18,650 at ₹ 159.50, which we had bought at ₹ 185.90, we would have incurred a total loss of ₹ 185.90-159.50=26.40×50=1,320.

Now the put of ₹ 18,500 which was sold at ₹ 151.60 would have to be bought at ₹ 173.35. In this test, we would have lost 173.35-151.60=21.75×50=1,087.50.

On the other hand, if we had sold the ₹ 18,450 put that we had bought at ₹ 135.65 at ₹ 154.70, we would have made a profit of ₹ 154.70-135.65=19.05×50=952.50.

Overall, according to this table, we would have incurred a loss of ₹ 32.50 plus brokerage and charges upon creating Iron Condor in intraday.

Type of Option	Strike Price	Sale/ Purchase	Premium at the Time of Sale or Purchase	Premium at the Time of Square Off	Profit/Loss on the Lot of 50
Call	18,600	Sale	212.70	184.25	1,422.50
Call	18,650	Purchase	185.90	159.50	-1,320.00
Put	18,500	Sale	151.60	173.35	-1,087.50
Put	18,450	Purchase	135.65	154.70	952.50
			Net Profit or Loss		**32.50**

Therefore, the Iron Condor strategy is not quite good for and successful in intraday because it mostly results in small loss or small profit in intraday. Overall, when brokerage and charges are added, it mostly results in a loss.

Now you will ask me - if this method is not so successful

then why did I waste your time? As a matter of fact, this method is not for intraday. Now your next question will be - if Iron Condor is not to be done in intraday, then where is it supposed to be done?

Should Iron Condor be done in monthly expiry?

Should Iron Condor be done in weekly expiry?

In order to explain this to you, I will give you the example of weekly expiry of Bank Nifty of Iron Condor, so that you can judge for yourself in which expiry it is better to buy Iron Condor.

I have not discriminated in any way in selecting the examples. I am writing this part of the book in July 2023. Hence, I have chosen expiry of July 6, 2023 for weekly expiry.

If we make an Iron Condor for Bank Nifty in the first week of July 2023, the expiry week from June 30 to July 6, 2023, then first of all, let us look at the levels of Bank Nifty of June 30, 2023 –

Date	Open	Highest	Lowest	Close
30-Jun-23	44,666.0	44,787.1	44,447.20	44,747.35

On Bank Nifty's expiry of July 6, 2023, the prices were as follows –

Date	Open	Highest	Lowest	Close
06-Jul-23	45,060.55	45,417.50	45,042.60	45,339.90

That is, Bank Nifty increased by 673.90 points in the entire week.

Suppose, to create an Iron Condor, we sold a call of 44,700 and bought a call of 44,800 as soon as Bank Nifty opened on July 6, 2023. Similarly, we sold a put of ₹ 44,600 and bought a put of ₹ 44,500. Now, if we had held it for the whole week till expiry, then on the day of expiry on July 6, 2023, we would have made profit and incurred loss as follows –

Type of Option	Strike Price	Sale/ Purchase	Premium at the Time of Purchase or Sale	Premium at the Time of Square Off	Profit/Loss on Lot of 25
Call	44,700	Sale	175	632.90	-11,447.50
Call	44,800	Purchase	149.85	541.95	9,802.50
Put	44,600	Sale	310	Worthless	7,750
Put	44,500	Purchase	265	Worthless	-6,625
				Total Profit or Loss	**-520**

From the above examples, you must have understood that in Iron Condor, we buy some cheaper (next out of the money) calls and puts with the same premium we get by selling call-puts.

That is, a part of the premium that we earned by selling calls and puts is used for buying calls and puts.

Therefore, we earn maximum profit only when all the call-puts that are bought and sold expire worthless.

This is possible only when the market remains range bound around 200 points in case of Nifty and around 400 points in case of Bank Nifty.

Now the monthly expiry is of a longer duration. Therefore, in this way in it, there is less possibility of the Nifty staying within the range of 200 points. But in weekly expiry we get only 5 days. Therefore, there is maximum possibility of the market remaining range bound in these 5 days. Therefore, Iron Condor should be made in Weekly Expiry.

In the above weekly expiry, Bank Nifty rose by 673.90 points. Therefore, there was a minor loss of ₹ 520. If it had increased by less than 400 points we would have been in profit. I have chosen the example honestly. That is why you could see an example of loss. But if you make Iron Condor in this way every week, then there will arise such occasions in the middle of the week, when your Iron Condor of 1 lot each of Bank Nifty can see a profit of more than ₹ 1,100. It is profitable to book it at that time. You can then create a new Iron Condor the next day with next week's expiry.

So, in short, the strategy here is -

1. Create one Iron Condor each in the weekly expiry of Nifty, Bank Nifty and Fin Nifty.

2. As the loss is limited in Iron Condor, there is no possibility of stop loss because you have limited your losses.

3. There is no need to wait till expiry to book profit in Iron Condor. Once your position becomes profitable, you can hold it with a trailing stop loss and book profits before expiry.

4. Even though this strategy has limited losses, do not forget to follow the 1-1 lot rule mentioned in the previous chapters of this book.

5. In Iron Condor, the optimum profit target is ₹ 1,100 for every 1 lot of Iron Condor. If you get a profit above ₹ 1,100 anytime in the middle of the week, then book it and create a new Iron Condor for the next week. There is not much need for stop loss in this. You can see that even when Bank Nifty moved above 600 points, our loss was limited to ₹ 520 only.

If you have more money, then invest it in other strategies. But if you create a position larger than 1 lot each simultaneously, then your chances of incurring losses increase because if your position becomes visible to big traders (so-called operators), they can get your stop loss hit.

I have written about this in detail in my book *41 Trading Tips*. For those who have not read that book, let me again explain as to how big operators in the market can easily see your position and get your stop loss hit very easily.

It is said that even walls can hear. Currently when trading is done via computer systems, your option positions can be easily viewed on the screen of your online trading service provider. You can also easily see the orders available in the market through market depth.

Through this, your online trading service provider can see your positions, whether you have taken margin positions or cash and carry. But apart from him, the broker, sub-broker, trading member etc. also can see your positions. It is difficult to say who can see your position. But in the computer age even this is not impossible.

You may think, 'Even if someone sees my orders and my trading positions, how does it matter to me?'

Have you ever played cards?

Did you let others see your cards?

What difference would it make to you if your playing cards were seen by your opponent?

I, the author of this book, am not 100 per cent sure about who can see your intraday option and margin positions and what are the potential chances for its misuse.

But if there is even 1 percent chance of this happening, then you are at risk. My wife even got a call from an online trading platform. A woman spoke, 'Seemaji, I see that you keep the stop loss very low, which often gets hit.' So, I asked her, 'Who is speaking?' She said, 'I am Seemaji's trading manager.' I said, 'What right do you have to see our positions and stop losses?'

She said, 'Our company has appointed client-wise relationship managers so that we can guide you to make money in trading. Seemaji's trading ID has been given to me. So, I am able to see her every trade, profit booking or loss booking and stop loss.'

Now imagine that you have bought 1,000 shares of a company on margin at a price of 1,043. You have kept a target of 1,048 and a stop loss of 1,038.

Therefore, if a big operator can see this position, then he knows how many orders are placed in the market at which prices. He can see that if he sells 5,000 shares of that company at same time, your stop loss will be hit, because if he sells 5,000 shares together, the price will fall to 1,043, 1,042, 1,041, 1,040... Thus, when it falls to 1,035, then your stop loss will hit at 1,038. At the same time, he will also buy back 5,000 shares.

His 5,000 shares were sold between ₹ 1,043 and ₹ 1,035. Many traders like you would like to close the position by selling shares at this price. If he buys back 5,000 shares from them for the amount between ₹ 1,035 and ₹ 1,038, he will make an enormous profit and you will incur a loss of ₹ 5,000 on 1,000 shares at ₹ 5 per share due to your stop loss being hit.

Now you may ask if this is so, then why is there a possibility of hitting the stop loss only in big positions and why the stop loss of our positions in 1 lot each cannot be hit?

The answer is simple and uncomplicated — the alleged

operator, if there is one, will focus on large positions; he is less likely to focus on small positions of 1-1 lot. Again, the stop loss that we have kept at ₹ 2,000 per lot is set far enough. This is not a small stop loss that the said operators can easily get triggered.

❑

12

My Scales Method for Options Trading

You must have seen a balance or a scale. When we go to the market to buy an item from a shopkeeper, he keeps a weight on one side of the scale and weighs the item of equal weight on the other side and then gives it to us.

In option trading as well, you can compare the option chain with scales. If a shopkeeper gives you goods weighing less than the weight on the scale, then you realise that the shopkeeper is being dishonest with you. On the other hand, if the shopkeeper gives you goods with a scale slightly tilted more than the weight, then you realise that the shopkeeper is trustworthy and is giving you the goods weighing just slightly more than the weight. In the same way, I am going to teach you a method to find out whether the market is going to rise or fall today by looking at the option chain like a scale.

Since it compares the option chain to the scales, I have named this method the Scales Method of Options Trading.

In the option chain, the strike price is given right in the middle. On the left side of it, the premium of call is given and on the right side, the premium of put is given.

To understand this better, look at picture number 3 carefully –

Option Chain

In this, in picture number 3, I have written - the strike price closest to the spot price. That means in order to use the scales method, we have to select the strike price which is closest to the spot price.

In the video of this method that I had posted on my YouTube channel, I had said that whatever call is in the money call based on the spot price, you have to select that strike price for the scales method.

Now, in the option market, the option chain is not considered on the basis of 'in the money call spot price' but on the basis of future price. So, my followers were confused after watching that video and were repeatedly commenting and asking, 'On the basis of spot price, call is not in the money or out of money. Since in the option, the future price is considered, should we consider the money call on the basis of spot price or on the basis of the future price?'

In fact, in the scales method, you always have to use the spot price. That is why, in this book, I have simplified the concept of the scales method.

Nifty/Bank Nifty/Fin Nifty – in whichever case you are using the scales method, you have to look at its spot price and select whichever strike price is closest to the spot price.

Now look carefully at the image number 4. I took this screen shot of the option chain of Nifty 50 of June 20, 2023 from my mobile at 10.30 am. The closing price of Nifty 50 on June 19, 2023 was 18,755.45 and on June 20, 2023, Nifty 50 opened at 18,752.35. That is, Nifty had a flat opening. When I took this screen shot at 10.30 on June 20, 2023, Nifty was trading at 18,671, which you can see in image number 4.

-83.80	50	240.50	241.05	700	18,550.00	700	50.40	50.55	3,500	16.95	50.60	10.20	14
-79.15	100	203.60	204.05	1,650	18,600.00	2,150	63.50	63.70	1,250	21.60	63.70	9.98	54,
-73.15	1,800	169.20	169.75	950	18,650.00	800	79.05	79.40	4,450	27.70	79.45	9.73	20
-67.85	3,050	138.00	138.10	1,300	18,700.00	400	97.75	97.85	100	32.95	97.75	9.51	81,
-61.15	2,300	110.40	110.75	1,150	18,750.00	750	119.75	120.00	250	39.40	119.70	9.26	28,
-53.60	350	86.10	86.30	200	18,800.00	750	145.65	146.05	400	47.35	145.75	9.02	57,
-46.50	950	65.80	66.00	200	18,850.00	750	174.55	175.00	800	54.85	175.00	8.73	7,0

That means the Nifty had fallen by 84.45 points from the previous day. At that time, a common trader would have naturally assumed that there would be a recession in the market today and he might have started making deals on the short side (bearish side).

Now let us try to find out using the scales method whether there was actually a higher possibility of the market falling or the market rising on that day.

According to the scales method, we have to select the strike price which is closest to the spot price of Nifty. The spot price of Nifty is 18,671, the strike of 18,650 is 21 points away from it and the strike of 18,700 is 29 points away from it. Therefore, the strike price of 18,650 is the closest price to the spot price of Nifty.

Now see the scale of premium for call and put at the strike price of ₹ 18,650.

Strike price of 18,650

Call Premium	**Put Premium**
Around 169.75	**Around 79.05**

So, which way are the scales tipped? Since the call premium is higher, the scales are naturally tilted in favour of calls.

Are people who are selling you puts stupid, who are selling you puts cheaper than calls even though the market has fallen and despite the market showing signs of a downtrend?

This is similar to the way a person puts bread in a cage to trap a mouse or a fisherman puts bait on his hook.

If there was a retail investor here, he would think that there is a recession in the market today, hence there is a possibility of the market falling and the put of ₹ 18,650 is also cheap. If I buy a call, I will have to pay a higher premium (169.75), but I will get a put for only 79.05. So, he buys the put.

Or if it were a short seller, he would have thought that since the call premium is high, let me short the call. But you should not do this at all. If the scales are tilted towards call, it is a clear indication that the market is more likely to rise today because big players are buying calls, the premium is higher.

Now, let us first talk about those who buy naked calls and puts. If you are a trader buying a naked (without any hedging) call-put, you should buy the call as per the scale, even if the premium is higher.

That day the market closed at 18,816.70 after making a low of 18,660. You can see that if you had bought a call of ₹ 18,650, you could have profited from this rise in the market.

Now you will ask that if we buy naked call-put based on the scales method, then what will be our stop loss and what will be our target?

The answer is that, first of all, I never encourage buying naked call-puts, and the scales method is not meant for buying call-puts directly without hedging.

Still if someone buys them, then they should buy in intraday only. There they should keep a stop loss of ₹ 2,000 for one lot and book profit in the last half hour of the market closure or they should book it whenever they get a profit above ₹ 1,100 on one lot.

Basically, you should use the scales method to decide whether to make a straddle or a strangle.

In the scales method, remember that if there is a difference of at least half a point in the premium of the call-put of the minimum difference between the strike prices of Nifty, Bank Nifty and Fin Nifty, only then it is considered that the scales are unbalanced.

For example, in Nifty, the strike price is maintained at a difference of 50 points each, then difference of half of 50 points, i.e. at least 25 points, must be there in the premium on both sides; only then the scales method is considered unbalanced. The greater the difference, the more accurately the scale method will work.

For example, the difference between the two strike prices in Bank Nifty and Fin Nifty is 100 points each, and in it, if the difference in call-put premiums is more than 50 points, only then is the scales method considered unbalanced.

Using the scales method, you can take trades in the following ways –

1. You can buy naked call or put (whichever side has higher premium) in intraday. But I do not recommend buying naked call-puts. In this also, whenever you buy, do not buy more than 1 call-put lot each. You should also keep a maximum stop loss of ₹ 2,000 per lot because the scale method is correct about 80-90 percent of the time, but it can also go wrong for the remaining 10-20 percent.
2. If the difference for Nifty is less than 25 points and if the difference for Bank Nifty/Fin Nifty is less than 50 points, then it is a sign of the market staying flat. The possibility of profit in making straddle is maximum on that day.
3. If the difference is far more than 25 points in Nifty and way more than 50 points in Bank Nifty, Fin Nifty, then it is profitable to make scale strangle on that day.

WHAT IS SCALES STRANGLE?

In a Balance Strangle, if the premium for call is high and that for put is low, as explained in the above example, the market is likely to rise. Therefore, you can sell put at the in the money strike price. But you should make the scales strangle by selling out-of-the-money calls at a strike price farther away, i.e. at least three steps away.

If it is the reverse, i.e. the premium in the put is high and the premium in the call is low, then sell the call at the in the money level and sell the out of the money put at least three steps lower. My methods also include the scales method. Check the scales daily between 10 am to 10.30 am and in case of imbalance, make 1-1 lot balance strangle. In this, keep the stop loss and target as explained in the previous chapters.

Furthermore, the scales method is mainly used in selling covered calls, which will be discussed in the next chapters.

❑

13

How to Earn Regular Monthly Income by Selling Covered Calls?

For option trading in covered call method, buy as many shares of whichever you consider to be good blue-chip companies or chip companies of Nifty Top 10 stocks in cash, which is at least their lot size. Then, every day, you should estimate that this stock cannot increase more than this today. For example, there is a lot of 250 shares of Reliance and you have gradually bought more than 250 shares of Reliance and the ongoing market price of Reliance is ₹ 2,750. You think that the price of this share will not go up or rise by more than ₹ 2,850 in intraday because in the last 3 months the price of a Reliance share has never gone up by more than ₹ 100 in a single day. So, if you sell one lot of Reliance at the strike price of ₹ 2,860 as soon as the market opens, and then if it does not gain as much momentum and the premium comes down as the closing time of the market approaches, then you can cover and take home your income for that day.

In the USA, the method of selling covered calls is being used by many retirees to generate regular monthly/weekly income. You will also be surprised to know that we Indians are way behind in this matter.

In the year 1975, a research article was published in America. This strategy was described for the first time in it. When you read this 1975 article titled 'Fact and Fantasy in the Use of Options' written by Fisher Black, you can understand how safe and successful the strategy which has been used by investors/traders around the world since 1975 is. To earn monthly income in covered call using this strategy, first of all you should hold shares of an established blue- chip company in demat purchased in cash in the same quantity as the lot of that share in the option.

For example, you want to earn regular income by making covered calls in Reliance, the company with the highest market cap in India. The lot size of the Reliance option is 250. You will be able to enjoy covered call only if you hold at least 250 shares of Reliance.

Now cover calls are also of two types –

1. Sell Right Covered Call
2. Buy Right Covered Call

1. **Sell Right Covered Call** - In this, the option writer sells the call option at a strike price below the market price of the shares he holds.

Let me explain to you with an example so that you will understand it clearly. Suppose the lot size of a company X is 500 shares and you have 500 shares of that company which you have purchased in cash.

Suppose the current ongoing market price of one share of this company is ₹ 1,400. There is a difference of ₹ 20 in the strike prices of this company in the option chain, that is, the strike prices are 1,280-1,300, 1,320-1,340, 1,360-1,380, 1,400-1,420, 1,440-1,460, 1,480-1,500.

Now, if such an investor writes or sells a call at ₹ 100 less than the market price of ₹ 1,400, i.e., ₹ 1,300 and at that time if the premium of in the money call of ₹ 1,300 is ₹ 180 at that time, then he will get a premium of 180×500=90,000.

In this sell right call, there is a condition of holding 500 shares. That is, once you have bought and held shares equal to the lot size, you can earn by writing calls with the security cover of these held stocks every month.

The market value of the shares held here at the time of writing the call was ₹ 1,400×500= ₹ 7 lakh. Now, if the expiry market price was ₹ 1,280, then at the rate of ₹ 120 per share, you actually incurred a loss of ₹ 120×500=60 thousand on the shares held. But by selling the call of ₹ 1,300, you had already received premium of ₹ 90,000, due to which you made a total profit of ₹ 30,000. If you had not written the call against the held shares, you would have incurred a loss of ₹ 60,000 due to a fall in their price, which you not only recovered by writing the call, but you also made a profit of ₹ 30,000.

(2) Now imagine what would have happened if the price of this share of expiry had come down to ₹ 1,100? Even then your written call of ₹ 1,300 would have expired worthless and you would have received the entire premium of ₹ 90,000. But this is the point where my stubborn followers argue with me and get upset with me, and abuse me in their comments on the YouTube videos that I have posted on this topic. You will ask me – why do they abuse or blame me? They have got ₹ 90,000,

then why do they abuse? They abuse because they say that as the market price of the 500 shares that they held fell by ₹ 300 per share, they actually incurred a loss of ₹ 1.50 lakhs, whereas the premium that they received was only ₹ 90,000. Therefore, they actually suffered a net loss of ₹ 1,50,000-90,000=60,000.

Such wise followers consider writing a naked call without holding shares in cash to be a more intelligent and wiser move. As I have often said, the options market is structured in such a way that money comes out of the pockets of small investors and goes into the pockets of big investors. Actually, firstly, small innocent investors who write naked calls do not have the ability to buy and hold 500 shares in cash, i.e. they do not have a capital of ₹ 7 lakh. So, they write naked calls without holding the shares bought in cash, and they write naked calls to satisfy their ego and justify themselves. When providentially, the market falls, they rejoice on getting the premium and start considering themselves wise. But just imagine what would have happened if the ₹ 1,300 call had been naked written with ₹ 180 premium and the price had gone up or risen to to ₹ 1,700? Those writing such naked calls would have incurred a loss of ₹ 400 per share and a loss of ₹ 2 lakhs on a lot of ₹ 500. Additionally, by deducting the premium of ₹ 90,000 that they received, they would have suffered a net loss of ₹ 1.10 lakh.

Here this loss is also compounded. That means if such a small investor earns a premium of ₹ 90,000 in a month, then he feels too confident about his intelligence, as a result of which he writes 5 naked calls instead of 1 naked call in the next month. By sheer luck, when he earns 40-50,000 in the second month as well, he becomes ecstatic. Then he writes 20 calls at the same time. Now prices go up swiftly, stop losses fail, market gap-up opens and a loss of ₹ 1 lakh per lot on 20 lots leads to a total loss of ₹ 20 lakhs.

Many times, investors trapped in such situations even commit suicide. Hence, I am strongly against writing naked calls. If it comes to writing a covered call, then first of all, the covered call shows your capacity. If you have 500 shares (minimum 1 lot size), then your capacity will be to write only 1 lot of call and you will not write more than 1 lot.

If you want to write 20 lots with covered call theory, then first you must have 500×20=10,000 shares, which is worth ₹ 1.40 crore and if you had the capacity to buy shares worth ₹ 1.40 crore, then you would have written 20 lots of call and the price would have increased from ₹ 1,400 to ₹ 1,700. If you had to pay ₹ 22 lakhs at the rate of ₹ 1.10 lakh per lot, then your held shares would have become worth ₹ 1.70 crore due to the increase in the price from ₹ 1,400 to ₹ 1,700 and you could have happily paid the difference by selling shares just worth 22 lakhs out of 1.70 crore.

Now, let us come back to the original point. Our original topic was that if we had held 500 shares bought at the market price of ₹ 1,400, taken a premium of ₹ 180, and had written 1 lot of a call of ₹ 1,300, and the market price had fallen by ₹ 300 to ₹ 1,100, then we would have incurred a loss of ₹ 500×300=1,50,000 on the holding, while the premium received would have been only ₹ 90,000, resulting in a net loss of ₹ 60,000.

The answer is as follows - First of all, if you had held only 500 shares and you had not hedged this position by writing a call, you would have incurred a loss of ₹ 1.50 lakhs, whereas by writing the call, and getting a premium of ₹ 90,000, at least this loss was reduced to ₹ 60,000. The second most important point is that the ₹ 90,000 premium that you received is the actual i.e., realized profit, whereas the loss incurred due to decline in the market value of the held shares is an imaginary, i.e. notional loss and unless you sell your shares, this loss is not a real loss.

Now you do not need to book loss by selling your held shares at ₹ 1,100. You keep the premium of ₹ 90,000 with you and write a call of ₹ 1,000 again next month. Now you will say that after writing a call of ₹ 1,000 in the following month, if the price increases to ₹ 1,500, then you will be trapped, that is, you will have to pay 500×500=2.50 lakhs.

But then the price of your held shares will also increase to ₹ 1,500, earning you a profit of ₹ 50,000 on your holding. You also have the premium of ₹ 90,000 that you earned last month. If you write a call of ₹ 1,000 also in this month, you may get an additional premium of ₹ 1,00,000. With this, you have already earned ₹ 50,000+90,000+1,00,000=2,40,000. Your actual loss will be only ₹ 10,000.

Although in this method, the losses are less as compared to naked calls, but still losses do occur. Therefore, this method is not 100 percent safe and I do not recommend my followers to write this type of covered call. The second option of covered call is more secure than this. So, let us discuss the second option.

2. **Buy Right Covered Call** – In this, the call writer writes a call above the current market price of the shares held by him. For example, an investor holds 500 shares of a company, whose current market price is ₹ 1,400. So, in this option the investor writes a call with a strike price above ₹ 1,400. Although 1,420, 1,440, 1,460, 1,480, 1,500, 1,520, 1,540—all are strike prices above 1,400, the call writer thinks that the chances of the price of share X going up from ₹ 1,400 to ₹ 1,500 in that month are very low. Therefore, he writes a

call of ₹ 1,500 against the 500 shares he holds at a premium of ₹ 36. He benefits from this in two ways –

1. He gets a premium at the rate of ₹ 36 per share, which comes to 500×36=18,000. Now if the price of that share remains between ₹ 1,400-1,500 till expiry, then the buyer of the call will not exercise his right to buy the share at the price of ₹ 1,500 and the call writer will get this ₹ 18,000 premium without buying or selling any share.
2. If the price of that share reaches 1,500 or 1,520 by expiry and the call buyer exercises his right, then the call writer will sell his held shares, which he had bought at a price of ₹ 1,400 (or bought at an even lower price and were already held), to the call buyer at the price of ₹ 1,500-1,520. This will earn him a profit of ₹ 100-120 per share. That means, apart from the profit of 500×100=50,000 or 120×500=60,000, he will also get a premium of 18,000.

Even though stock options trades in India are now settled through physical delivery, you can still avail the difference in cash if you sell your contract shortly before expiry. Therefore, if a call of ₹ 1,500 is sold, the call writer does not have to pay anything at the price of ₹ 1,500. At the price of ₹ 1,520, he will have to pay a difference of 20×500=10,000, whereas the premium received was ₹ 18,000. Therefore, ₹ 8,000 will be saved in premium and he will not have to buy or sell any shares.

Now let me tell you the point on which objections are raised against me. My followers write on YouTube - 'This method is very risky. If the price of that share goes up or rises to 1,600 and we sell a call of 1,500, then at the rate of 1,600-1,500 = 100 rupees per share, there will be a loss of 50,000 on a lot of

500.' So, my followers write, 'This is a very stupid method. Therefore, do not mislead us needlessly.'

Please note, you have 500 shares purchased at the rate of ₹ 1,400. When you write a covered call of ₹ 1,500 against them, your profit of ₹ 100 is secured. You made ₹ 100 profit between ₹ 1,500 and ₹ 1,600 and that is what you gave to the call buyer.

For example - in fact, when the price becomes ₹ 1,600, then you will sell your 500 shares of ₹ 1,400 at the price of ₹ 1,600 and book a profit of ₹ 1,00,000 on 500 shares at ₹ 200 per share and you will get a premium of ₹ 18,000. Out of this ₹ 1,18,000, you will pay ₹ 50,000 which is the difference between ₹ 1,500-1,600. Your net profit still remains ₹ 1,18,000-50,000=68,000. When I give them the answer, they say – 'But after that, our holding shares are sold. Therefore, your statement that this can generate income every month is nonsense. Once we have sold 500 shares, what will we do next month?'

What can I say now? People abuse even after making a secured profit of ₹ 68,000 because their shares were sold and out of ₹ 1,18,000 profit, ₹ 50,000 profit had to be paid to the call buyer. The pain of this outweighs the joy of the remaining earnings of ₹ 68,000. Then, they are also disheartened as to how they will write the covered call next month.

Through my years of research, I have found two solutions for this. The first solution is to plant a money tree, about which you have read in my previous book *'How to Plant a Money Tree Through Option Trading'*. The second solution is to sell share genius covered calls, which will be explained in the next chapter.

❑

14

Sell Share Genius Covered Calls Instead of Poor Man's Covered Calls

The capital required for the covered call which I mentioned in the previous chapter is ₹ 7-8 lakhs, which a common retail investor does not have.

So, some investors developed a certain strategy which was similar to covered calls, but which required lower capital. It is called Poor Man's Covered Call Strategy.

Poor Man's Covered Call is also called 'Synthetic Covered Call'.

There are two steps in selling a poor man's covered call—

1. Buy an in-the-money call with a longer expiry period.
2. Sell an out-of-the-money call with a nearby expiry.

This method is more popular in foreign countries, where stock options with expiry of 6 months, 9 months, 12 months are also available. So, if a person wants to buy 250 shares (equivalent to one lot) of a blue chip, say Reliance (in the context of India) for a covered call in cash, he will need a capital of ₹ 6,87,500 for 250 shares at the market price of ₹ 2,750. Therefore, instead of selling covered calls, if he wants to take advantage of the poor man's covered calls, he buys in-the-money calls of such blue-chip shares with expiry after one year, which is comparatively cheaper. Even if the premium on such a call is ₹ 400, he gets the position by paying the total amount of 400×250=1 lakh, whereas if he had bought 250 shares in the cash market, he would have paid ₹ 6,87,500.

Some people also create long positions by paying one-third margin in futures. This is also called synthetic covered call or poor man covered call.

They then continue to earn premium by buying future positions of long expiry created in this way or in the money calls with long expiry and selling out of the money calls with nearby expiry.

But this strategy is not as simple as it appears. In fact, in India, in the first place, stock options with long term options of more than 3 months are not available.

And then, even if long-term options are found in Nifty etc. instead of stocks, there is not much liquidity in long-term calls in most of the blue chips, that is, there are fewer call sellers.

Even if you are fortunate enough to buy an in the money call in a long-term option, its premium is so high that you will not be able to earn that much premium by selling the calls in the nearest expiry.

So overall, Poor Man's Covered Call is not a good strategy in the Indian context. In this, I have mostly seen losses. I often joke that selling a poor man's covered call keeps you poor. However, actually the Poor Man's Covered

Call is meant for the poor man so that the poor man can avail the benefit of the covered call in it at a lower premium. But once I saw a stone-hearted doctor (whose name I will not reveal) arguing with one of his poor patients over the bill saying that his hospital was not meant for the poor. He said that if he was poor, he should have gone to a government hospital. I remembered the heartless dialogue of that doctor because the option market is also not meant for the poor. If you are poor, then you can opt for SIP in relatively safe investment vehicles like ETFs etc. The structure of the options market is such that the money comes out of the pockets of those with low margin and goes to those with high margin. So, overall, since the options market is not meant for the poor, I would advise you not to use covered calls at all.

Hence, I would recommend you to use Share Genius Covered Call instead of Poor Man Covered Call in intraday.

In this, if you want to make Share Genius covered call in Nifty, then buy 1.20 times of the shares required for covered call of Nifty ETF in intraday.

Let me explain to you by giving the example of Nifty Seed.

See picture number 5 given below -

-83.80	50	240.50	241.05	700	**18,550.00**	700	50.40	50.55	3,500	16.95	**50.60**	10.20	[illegible]
-79.15	100	203.60	204.05	1,650	**18,600.00**	2,150	63.50	63.70	1,250	21.60	**63.70**	9.98	54,
-73.15	1,800	169.20	169.75	950	**18,650.00**	800	79.05	79.40	4,450	27.70	**79.45**	9.73	2
-67.85	3,050	138.00	138.10	1,300	**18,700.00**	400	97.75	97.85	100	32.95	**97.75**	9.51	81,
-61.15	2,300	110.40	110.75	1,150	**18,750.00**	750	119.75	120.00	250	39.40	**119.70**	9.26	28,
-53.60	350	86.10	86.30	200	**18,800.00**	750	145.65	146.05	400	47.35	**145.75**	9.02	57,
-46.50	950	65.80	66.00	200	**18,850.00**	750	174.55	175.00	800	54.85	**175.00**	8.73	7,0

This is a picture of Nifty 50 monthly expiry option chain taken from my mobile on June 20, 2023 at 10.30 am.

In this, the spot price ran at ₹ 18,671. However, in the option chain, in the money call-puts are determined not on the basis of spot price but on the basis of future price.

But as I have mentioned earlier, in our methods we determine in the money call-puts based on the spot price. Therefore, wherever in the money call-put is mentioned in my methods, you should understand that it is based on spot price only.

So, based on the spot price of 18,671, the call of ₹ 18,650 was in the money call. As per image no. 5, around 10.30 am on June 20, 2023, the premium of this call was trading at 169.20.

That is, if you had sold a call of ₹ 18,650 here in intraday, you would have received a premium of ₹ 169.20×50=8,460 on the call of ₹ 18,650.

Now look at the following picture number 6, which I took from my mobile on the same day, i.e. June 20, 2023 at 3.18 pm.

.04	257.90	15.20	250	257.50	258.35	750	18,650.00	2,200	40.95	41.20	3,000	-10.75	41.00
.54	217.55	11.60	50	217.85	218.00	300	18,700.00	2,100	50.95	51.05	450	-13.80	51.00
.22	179.05	7.35	300	178.80	179.30	1,000	18,750.00	1,050	64.15	64.40	600	-16.05	64.25
97	147.00	7.05	50	147.15	147.20	100	18,800.00	150	80.55	80.75	1,900	-17.65	80.75
57	116.40	4.10	500	116.70	116.95	700	18,850.00	1,050	98.50	98.75	850	-21.15	99.00
33	89.85	2.60	250	89.85	90.15	400	18,900.00	50	123.30	123.50	250	-21.05	123.65
09	66.60	0.35	50	66.90	67.05	150	18,950.00	150	149.55	150.05	50	-23.00	149.80

If at the time (at 10.30 am) of selling the call of ₹ 18,650 the market was at 18,671, then at 3.18 pm the market had risen to 18,825.10. Now as per the above picture number 6, you would have to buy your shorted call of ₹ 18,650 by paying a premium of ₹ 258.35. That is, in this trade you would have incurred a loss of ₹ 258.35-169.20=89.15 per Nifty share, which would have resulted in a total loss of ₹ 89.15×50=4,457.50 on a lot size of 50.

Most naked call sellers incur substantial losses in this manner. Although loss is never good, it is acceptable for naked call sellers because God is very merciful. By making you incur a loss for selling naked call, the merciful God wants to make you understand that selling naked call is risky, hence you should never sell naked call-put.

That day at 10.30 am, the market was down by 84.45 points and the premium on call was also higher than that on put. So, any greedy investor could have fallen into the trap of selling naked calls.

Now let us see what would have happened if this call of ₹ 18,650 was sold in intraday as a Share Genius covered call?

In this, first of all, you have to buy some units of Nifty Seed ETF to cover this call.

You must have seen that when ETFs based on Nifty and Bank Nifty are opened, they are offered at very high prices. This happens because when the market opens, many market players who sell covered calls buy Nifty and Bank Nifty ETFs to cover their calls.

Now, since the price of ETFs is higher as soon as the market opens, I have chosen for you a time of about 1 hour after the market opens to sell Share Genius Covered Calls.

100 units of Nifty Seed are approximately equal to 1 Nifty. You may say that when Nifty was at 18,671, the market price of Nifty Seed was 205.30. According to this, 205.30×100=20,530 becomes the price of Nifty.

The reason for this is that there is a difference in the premium in Nifty Seed depending on the cash component like dividend, tracking error and demand and supply. But you have to roughly assume that to hedge one Nifty, you will have to buy 100 units of Nifty Seed.

Now, as I told you earlier that for Share Genius covered call, you have to buy 1.20 times of the ETF intraday. So, for 1 Nifty at the rate of ₹ 100, you had to buy 100×50=5,000 ETF units for 50 Nifty. But since we have to buy 1.20 times, we will buy 5,000×1.20=6,000 units in intraday.

Here, we also want to sell covered call in intraday only. Therefore, we will also buy Nifty Seed ETF in intraday only. The only way to reduce the margin in this method is that we sell a new covered call every day intraday. So, firstly, there is an opportunity to sell calls at different levels every day and secondly, with respect to the 1.20 times the lot size of the ETF that we require to cover this call, we also require less margin if we buy it for intraday only.

Buying ₹ 6,000 Nifty Seed ETF in intraday would have required a margin of around ₹ 2,46,360, which you can see in the following image number 7.

Now even if you had sold a call of Nifty at ₹ 18,650, you would have required a margin of around ₹ 1 lakh. That is, for setup of Share Genius Covered Call in intraday you require a margin of around ₹ 3.50 lakhs.

Now, if you had bought 6,000 Nifty seeds at the rate of ₹ 205.30, then at the time of market closing that day, the price of Nifty seeds at 3.16 was ₹ 206.49, which you can see in the following image number 8.

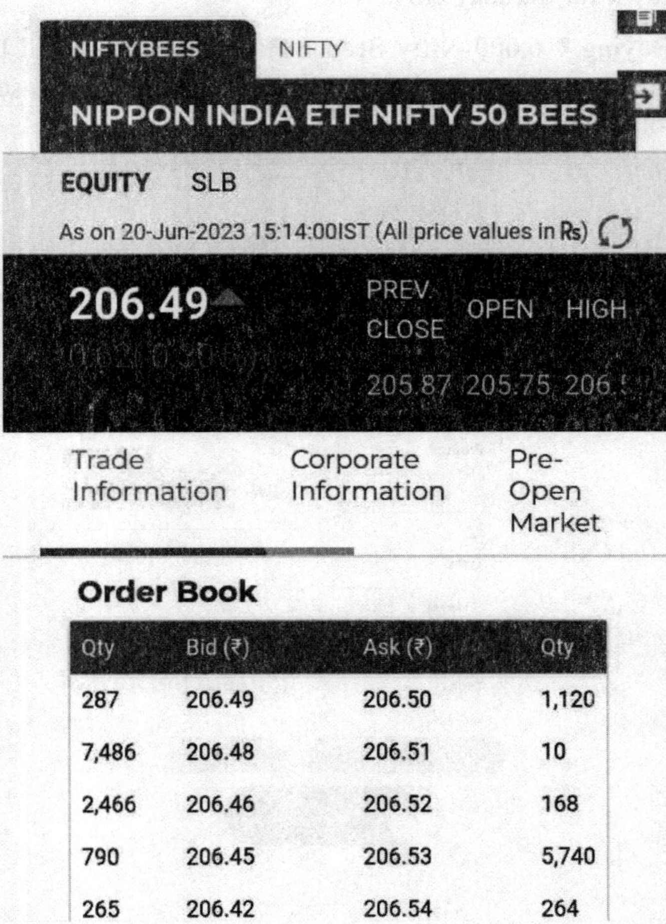

Qty	Bid (₹)	Ask (₹)	Qty
287	206.49	206.50	1,120
7,486	206.48	206.51	10
2,466	206.46	206.52	168
790	206.45	206.53	5,740
265	206.42	206.54	264

Now, at the rate of ₹ 206.49-205.30=₹ 1.19 per unit, you would have made a profit of ₹ 1.19×6,000=7,140 on 6,000 units. From this, after deducting the loss of selling calls of ₹ 18,650, the net profit would have been ₹ 7,140-4,457.50=2,682.50.

To give you an example, I have selected a day when the market had risen. Similarly, even if the market had fallen, you would have made a profit by selling the call. But the price of Nifty seed in cash would have fallen less because some people would have been buying ETFs for investment, too. Therefore, mostly the difference has been seen compared to the decline in the value of the ETF. Hence, even if the market falls, your chances of making overall profit remain high.

By selling this type of Share Genius covered call daily in intraday, you will make a profit on most of the days, but sometimes there can be loss, too.

In this, the formula of profit and stop loss is the same simple one that you should not sell more than 1 covered call in Nifty's intraday. However, if you have more margin, then you can sell 1 covered call each of Nifty and Bank Nifty. Keep a gap of 1 hour between selling of both. For example, if you sell Nifty covered call at 10.30, then sell Bank Nifty at 11.30.

Whenever the total profit-loss setup of your Share Genius Covered Call starts appearing in loss above ₹ 2,000, you should consider it as stop loss and exit both the positions.

Here both the positions covered call and ETF intraday overall will have stop loss above ₹ 2,000 and both the positions overall will have a profit target above ₹ 2,000. Otherwise, you have to collect whatever profit or loss occurs in the last half hour of the market and leave.

I hope that you have understood the Share Genius Covered Call Strategy.

Share Genius Covered Call is more effective compared to Poor Man's Covered Call. You can make estimate in this regard through paper trading.

❑

15

Experiences of Some of My Readers About the Methods Described in This Book

In the initial years of my life, I worked as a teacher in a private educational institution for about 3 years and 8 months. I have always given priority to morality, ideals and values in my life. At that time, since I wanted to improve my financial circumstances, I used to give tuitions in science and mathematics to children at my home even after my working hours at the institution.

But I did not get trapped by the greed that children should come to my house for tuition and give up my ideals, values and morals. That is why, I would give exactly the same notes and teach exactly the same lessons in the tuition that I gave in the school class. So, some children from rich families would advise me – 'Sir, we attend your tuitions because we want to learn something better and different from what you teach in the class so that we can get ahead of the poor classmates who do not take tuitions from you. But you teach the same things in the tuitions that you teach in the class. So, what benefit do we get by taking tuitions from you?

I would answer them in this manner: My conscience does not allow me to teach well at home and badly at school. You may or may not take my tuitions, I may not have enough to eat. But I cannot ignore my conscience'. Similarly, most of the methods that I have explained in this book have been already been taught by me through my free videos on my channel on YouTube. If you feel unhappy that whatever is explained in this book has already been mentioned in the YouTube videos, then you may give a lower rating to my book. However, it also has its benefits.

After I uploaded the videos that are free of charge on YouTube, millions of my followers have tried these methods. They tried these methods through paper trades and have shared their experiences with me. So, I am sharing some of these selected experiences with you in this book as they may prove useful to you.

Dr. Paresh Kumar Singh is one of my followers and friends. He runs a coaching centre in Varanasi. In his e-mail, he has suggested that the possibility of profit can be higher if the following modifications are made in the Owl Strangle Method:

1. CE and PE should be sold at least +/- 2 percent above the CMP of Nifty 50. For example, if Nifty is at 19,500 at 10 am, I will sell 19,900 CE and 19,100 PE at the end of the month, the expiry of which call-put I sell should be at least 14 days after my purchase.
2. Use the strike price which has the same delta value of CE and PE.
3. I sold both CE and PE after 10 am but before 10.15 am to avoid sudden fluctuations in the first 45 minutes. Then to

avoid the sharp fluctuations in Nifty in the last 45 minutes, I covered them before 2.45 pm.

You can verify Dr. Paresh Kumar Singh's suggestions through paper trade.

Another follower of mine, Mr. Sunil Shukla, writes –

Sir,

I worked for two weeks after watching your video about the scales method, due to which I made 100 per cent profit in trades. As of now, since I do not have much confidence, I am not able to stay in profit for long. That is why I made profit in the last 10 days. But if I had continued longer as per your method, I would have made even more profit. I am telling you in detail how much profit I made every day. This method of yours works well. Thank you very much –

I started with ₹ 5,500.

Profit on the first day - ₹ 2,500

Profit on the second day - ₹ 1,250

Profit on the third day - ₹ 700

Profit on the fourth day - ₹ 1,500

Profit on the fifth day - ₹ 1,800

Profit on the sixth day - ₹ 1,000

There was a loss of ₹ 600 on the seventh day, which was due to my mistake as I did not wait for the stop loss.

Profit on the eighth day - ₹ 1,400

Profit on the ninth day - ₹ 1,525

Profit on the tenth day (today) - ₹ 500

Similarly, my follower Mr. Tarun Nayyar from Batala, Punjab wrote that he back-tested my scales method for 4-5 days in intraday. on June 30, 2023, at 9.40 am, Mr. Tarun Nayyar saw the scales at 19,050 with the premium on call around ₹ 128 and the premium on put around ₹ 67. Therefore, at 9.44 am, as the scales were unbalanced, he bought two lots of call worth ₹ 19,050. He kept a target of 25 points and a stop loss of 20 points. But when he made a profit of 22 points, he quickly booked the profit and earned a profit of ₹ 2,200.

Similarly, on July 3, 2023, Mr. Tarun Nayyar again made a profit of ₹ 2,245, of which he has also sent me two screen shots. You can see both the screenshots in the following image number 9 and image number 10 –

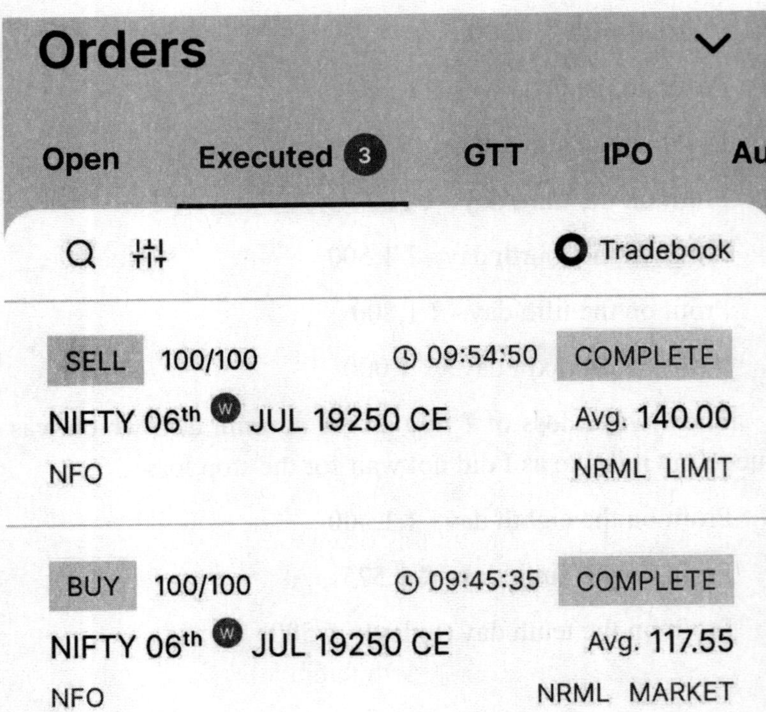

NIFTY 06th W JUL 19250 CE

NFO 144.30 +93.95 (+186.59%) NRML

Position details

Avg. price	0.00
Net qty.	0
Carry forward qty.	0
Day's P&L	2,245.00
P&L	2,245.00

Buys

Buy Qty.	Buy price	Buy value
100	117.55	11,755.00

Sells

Sell Qty.	Sell price	Sell value
100	140.00	14,000.00

Another follower of mine, Mustafa Bohra, wrote: ‘I am connected through your channel. You shared this scales method 10 days ago and I have been paper trading it for about 6 days’.

I have obtained very accurate results.

I feel doubtful about this when the difference on both sides of the call and put is almost the same. It is difficult to estimate at that time.

I have observed two more things with this.

PCR of an option chain and 3 candles on the chart is being more accurate than that.

Thus, you can also benefit from the experiences of the followers mentioned above about how to use these methods in practice and how to set target and stop loss points in these methods.

❑

16

How to Sell Gold and Silver Covered Calls for Option Trading in Commodities

For option trading, it is not necessary that to do option trading in the stock market only. You can also do option trading in commodities like gold and silver. To do option trading in commodity gold and silver, you do not need to open a separate account in MCX. You can also do gold and silver option trading on MCX with your existing demat account.

Most brokers provide this type of facility, in which you can also trade in commodities on MCX like share trading on NSE and BSE. For example, suppose you have an account with Zerodha broker. If you have not selected the commodity option at the time of opening the account, then you will have to activate the commodity option by going to the console option of Zerodha. After that you can search for call-puts of the commodity in the same way as you search for normal call-puts in the watchlist. For example, to search for a silver call, you have to type SILVER CE 72,000 in the watchlist, then in the drop-down menu, you will see the strike price of the call available in the silver futures market. After selecting the options and adding them to your watchlist, you can do option trading in gold and silver as per the principles explained in this book.

Just as you can see the option chain of Nifty and Bank Nifty etc. on the website of NSC, similarly you can also see the option chain of gold, silver etc. by visiting the website of MCX. Currently the volumes in commodities like gold and silver are very low. However, as you have read in my book, according to my principles, you have to buy only one lot or sell only one lot. So, you get at least this much volume in MCX.

Since the volatility in gold and silver is very low and there is also physical delivery, most of the major jewellers dealing in gold and silver take positions in gold and silver on MCX.

In the stock market, you also come across new and clumsy investors in options trading, who increase volumes unnecessarily and just as a drowning person holds on to his rescuer and also causes him to drown, in the same way, in options trading in the stock market, sometimes you too may get confused and incur losses due to indiscriminate trades done by clueless investors. But I have seen that only experienced people trade in gold and silver on MCX. Therefore, you can trade easily in it with small profits and small losses. If you do not have experience in option trading in gold and silver, then you should first try paper trading for a few days and only then get into real trading.

Now, I will tell you about how you can use Share Genius Covered Call in Gold and Silver because according to me, using Covered Call in Gold and Silver is the safest strategy.

Just like you were taught in the previous chapter about using covered call by buying 1.20 times the units of Nifty ETF, similarly gold and silver ETFs are also available for it. You can use covered calls in them by buying 1.20 times the lot size. The lot size of Mini Gold in the option is currently 100 grams and the lot size of Silver Mini Futures is currently 5kg. The exchange keeps changing the lot sizes. Therefore, you should keep in mind the current lot size while accumulating units of gold-silver ETFs for covered calls.

It is even safer and easier to make profits by selling covered calls in gold and silver option trading. In gold and silver option trading, the expiry is at an interval of 3 months and deals for about 9 months or up to the next 3 months are also available.

Owing to low volume in gold and silver options trading, you cannot do intraday trading in them. Therefore, if you want to make a covered call in gold and silver, then you should use covered call for the entire month. Therefore, I suggest that you should buy gold and silver ETFs using the money tree method as explained in my book '*How to Plant a Money Tree with Option Trading*' so that instead of buying all at once, when you accumulate units gradually while earning profits through the money tree method, the average price of your units will also be less.

Therefore, you should use covered calls in gold and silver based only on the money tree method. Only then can you get the full benefit of option trading in gold and silver.

Option trading also takes place in the currency market just like option trading in gold and silver. From this chapter, you must have learnt that in gold and silver options trading, I recommend selling covered calls using only the money tree method. In the next chapter, you will be given information about currency options trading in the currency market.

❑

17

Earning Regular Income from Options Trading in the Forex Market

Currency trading is also known as Forex trading. Forex trading basically means buying and selling of currency. Forex trading is one of the largest financial markets in the world. More than 5 trillion is traded daily in Forex. Forex trading takes place all over the world. So, Forex trading takes place 24 hours a day in some country or the other in the world.

In fact, I believe that option trading in gold, silver and currency is much safer than option trading in stocks because firstly, it is universal all over the world and their prices are well linked with each other. For example, you must have seen that in gold and silver, ups and downs occur simultaneously. Similarly, the currency of each country is also linked to the currency of other countries. Then, the fluctuations in gold and silver also have an impact on Forex because every country has gold and silver reserves and on the basis of that, the international valuation of that country's currency is done.

Currency trading in India is regulated by RBI and SEBI because currency trading affects the economy of the country. If the value of rupee starts falling beyond a certain limit, then RBI intervenes and starts selling dollars, which stops the decline in the value of rupee. Therefore, since there is not much fluctuation in currency trading, there is less possibility of rapid profit loss in it.

As there are no sharp losses, currency trading is a better option for traders who do not want to take much risk by trading in futures and options. Apart from investors and traders, many big companies, central banks of different countries, travellers travelling from one country to another deal in the currency market.

Currency trading in India started just a few years ago. Earlier, if you wanted to trade in international currency pairs like dollar and pound from India, you were required to open your trading account with a broker firm abroad.

Typically, you would find such brokers abroad in countries like Egypt or Greece. After opening the account, you would then be required to convert your money into dollars and wire transfer it to the account of the broker in the foreign country. After that, you would be able to trade only on the basis of guidance given by the broker. But now NSE has arranged the complete setup for currency trading and you can easily trade options and futures in currency from your demat account in India.

Companies also enter into deals in the currency market to hedge their positions. Currency trading in India takes place through NSE. Currency trading takes place in pairs, for example, Dollar-INR, Dollar-Euro, Euro-Pound, Yen-INR etc. In India you can trade Forex in the following currency pairs:

1. USD–INR
2. EURO–INR
3. GBP–INR
4. JYP–INR
5. GBP–USD
6. EUR–USD
7. USD–JPY

Now, if you trade in USD/INR pair, then USD will be called the 'Base Currency' and INR will be called the 'Quotation Currency'. You can buy USD/INR futures lots. In this, the lot size is $1,000. Around the world, the value of currencies is written up to the fourth decimal place. This is called PIP or 'Percentage in Points'. For USD/INR, the base of PIP is 0.0025, which means that the minimum price difference will be in 0.0025 and prices will move in multiples of it. At present, the expiry of currency futures is on every Friday and deals with weekly expiry are available in it. But you can also make deals for a period of up to one year. For example, in May 2022, in USD/INR futures, the lot with expiry of May 27, 2022 was trading at 77.5725, hence, at the same time, the lot with expiry of April 26, 2023 was also trading at 80.0775 and it had a volume of 15,314 lots by 1 pm.

This capital is the main reason why trading in currency futures is popular. The leverage in this is very high and one can get positions in it at only 2.5 percent margin. For example, if you had bought one lot of $1,000 at 77.57250 with expiry of May 27, 2022, the total value of your deal would have been ₹ 77,572.50 and you would have got a position in 1 lot at a margin of only 2.5 percent, i.e. ₹ 1,938.17. If its price had gone up by just 0.20 points, i.e., if it had become 77.7725, then you would have earned ₹ 200 per lot of 1,000, and after deducting brokerage of ₹ 40 from ₹ 200, the balance of ₹ 160 would have remained.

Currency futures have low risk as their prices change very slowly. But on the basis of this, it cannot be said that there is no risk at all. Sometimes there can be a big move in them, too and you can incur a big loss. But through derivative deals in equity and commodity, these have the lowest risk.

If you want to earn from currency trading, then the Calendar Spread Method is a good method for it. In this, both buy and sell positions are created in different expiry months.

You must have understood what my preference is. I have already explained my share trading methods to you in this book. Among these, Owl Method, Scales Method, Money Tree and Share Genius Covered Call are the methods invented by me in which my followers have been trading for a long time.

Similarly, for trading in gold and silver, I prefer the money tree method and for trading in the Forex market, I prefer only the calendar spread method.

Calendar Spread Method – I will try to explain the Calendar Spread Method to you with a very simple example. On NSE, on May 9, 2022, the USD/INR price per rate of May 27, 2022 was 77.6075 and the future rate for next month's expiry of June 28, 2022 was 77.8575.

Generally speaking, the premium for futures with longer duration is higher and the premium for futures with shorter duration is lower. Now, in this, you have to buy the lot with expiry of May 27, 2022 and sell the lot with expiry of June 28, 2022. With this, your position is hedged. Of course, now the price of US dollar increases/decreases. So, you will make profit in one position and loss in the other. But you have already bought and sold lots with a difference of 0.25 and made arbitrage. So, overall, your chances of profit will be higher.

While making arbitrage in this, keep in mind that you have to make an arbitrage only when the overall difference is 0.25 points or more. While making arbitrage, do not consider only LTP, but also look at the actual ask price and bid price and then only take the trade because it should not happen that instead of the price at which you place the order, the ask price and the bid price are different and the trade is executed at a different price.

For a better understanding of the profit in calendar spread, you should do paper trade, that is, you should note down imaginary trades on paper and check every day as to what would have happened if you had taken the real trade. Once you gain a good understanding with the help of the paper trade, you can create real trades.

How to earn regular income for daily household expenses from currency trading?

The caption 'Earning Income for Daily Household Expenses from Currency Trading' must have sounded very attractive! I regularly get many e-mails where my followers ask me to advise them on some method by which they can earn ₹ 400-500 daily in intraday so that their household expenses are taken care of. In fact, people in foreign countries actually do this, and after watching such videos of foreigners, the same desire is aroused in our minds.

If you want to do this, then the option of intraday in equities or intraday in options etc. is riskier. In comparison to them, making calendar spreads in currency has the lowest risk. Only about ₹ 4,000 to ₹ 5,000 of margin is required to create a calendar spread.

Since, no business gives guarantee of returns, the method that I will explain here also neither gives any guarantees nor it is risk free. However, it has higher earning potential and lower risk compared to equity. Therefore, use this method as per your discretion. Please do not hold me responsible if you incur any loss on account of your greed or irresponsible use of this method.

In this method, calendar spread is made in all those currency pairs with high volume of currency in intraday, whose price difference is more than 0.25. That is, a lot of currency in the futures with expiry of this month is bought and the lot of futures with expiry of next month is sold at minimum 0.25 more. It is all right if the difference is more than this, but it should not be less than this.

No more than one lot is taken in any position and these positions are also held in intraday only. If there is a total profit of ₹ 200-400 in all the positions after brokerage, then all the positions are exited together.

I will not explain calendar spread in currency in much detail in this book because as I have already mentioned this book is written only for advanced options traders, wherein I am assuming that you already know the basics of options trading. However, if you have any problems, you can search and watch some videos about calendar spreads on YouTube.

Overall, currency trading is the most widespread and most modern form of trading. To earn through this, you need to develop a sense to find business opportunities. In this, options are also traded and like equity, call-puts of currency are also sold. In this, you can also trade in options and buy lots of a currency pair in the future and sell covered calls in the option. This is called 'Poor Man's Covered Call' or 'Synthetic Covered Call', which I have already explained earlier in this book.

Since there is no ETF of the currency in the stock market yet, reserve banks all over the world, like RBI in India, are seriously considering launching their own digital currencies. After that, it is possible that you will be able to hold digital forms of dollars etc. in your demat account in the same way as you hold shares. After the arrival of digital currency, their ETFs may also be introduced.

But till this happens, you will have to use the poor man's covered calls or synthetic covered calls in currency, where instead of holding the actual currency, you hold a lot of the future and sell the call at the higher level in the option.

❑

18

Vertical Strangle Method

While reading this book, you must have realized that most of the methods mentioned in the book are new to you and you have not read them in any other book before. This is because I share my original research with you through books. If you type 'option trading strategy PDF' and search on the internet, then you will see many free PDF books opening in front of you, whereby you will find many option trading strategies in PDF books of 40 to 100 pages. However, in each of those books you will find that the old methods of option trading like Straddle, Strangle, Bull Call Spread, Bear Call Spread, Covered Call, Iron Condor, Butterfly etc. are only described. These books do not explain to you any method or research as to how to use them.

I am fond of reading books. I have also bought many books on option from Amazon and read them on Kindle. But I was surprised to see that in the 300–400-page books written by foreign authors that I have read after paying astronomical sums, most of the pages contain the same basic knowledge about what is straddle, what is a covered call, etc. They just give some definitions, description of charts, etc., and then some examples. And almost everyone talks about the risk-reward that if you are bullish towards the market then the reward is high, if you feel that the market is going to fall then the reward is high, etc.

Just think about it. If we could know whether the market would rise or fall today, then why would we need to read books? In that case, we would have been able to earn money easily even without books and knowledge. The tricky issue is that the movement of the market is uncertain and we do not know whether the market will fall or rise today! That is why we need so many methods. In a nutshell, I am giving you so many details because I have never been satisfied with books which teach only the basics. Hence, I did not want my book to end up becoming a similar type of basic book that described methods and charts.

I sincerely wish that only beneficial and my tried and tested techniques should be described in my book. Well, now I have come to the last part of the book. I was still not satisfied. I felt that there was still some new topic that I needed to talk about. Initially, I thought of talking about the call-put spread and the 4-stroke method. But then I realized that I had already described these methods in my previous books. In that case, my followers who read all my books would be disappointed that I am repeating the same methods which I have described in the previous books.

Then I remembered one remaining method, which is my favourite method. The name of this method is – 'Vertical Strangle'. Do not panic after reading the name! This method is very easy and like owl strangle, this is also my original method. That is why you will not find it anywhere else.

Now let's quickly start the method. In a way, this method is an advanced version of my 4-stroke method. In order to understand this easily, I would like you to look at the data of Nifty from July 17, 2023 to July 21, 2023.

You can see this data in Table 11 –

Date	Opened	Highest	Lowest	Closed
Jul 17, 23	19,612.15	19,731.85	19,562.95	19,711.45
Jul 18, 23	19,787.5	19,819.45	19,690.2	19,749.25
Jul 19, 23	19,802.95	19,851.7	19,727.45	19,833.15
Jul 20, 23	19,831.7	19,991.85	19,758.4	19,979.15
Jul 21, 23	19,800.45	19,887.4	19,700	19,745

Now on the day that you want to use this method, make a vertical line from the data of the previous day as follows –

Strike price above previous day's high

↕

Previous day's high

↕

Previous day's low

↕

Strike price below the previous day's low

Do not panic. Let us try to draw this line in practice as well. Then you will understand everything. For example, if we want to execute this method on July 18, 2023, then the vertical line made from the data of July 17, 2023 will appear as follows –

19,750

↕

19,731.85

↕

19,562.95

↕

19,550

You can see that to create this line, I wrote the previous day's high, i.e., July 17, 2023's high which was 19,731.85. Then I wrote above that the strike price of 19,750, which was above the previous day's high. Similarly, in place of the previous day's lowest level, I wrote 19,562.95, which was the low of July 17. Then I wrote 19,550 in place of the strike price below that.

So, now you see, how easy it is to make this vertical line! But when you will learn trading related to it, you will say that this is the simplest but most powerful chart in the world.

Now after forming this line, you can use this method only if the market opens somewhere between the high and low of the previous day. Otherwise, you have to postpone the use of this method till the next day.

As you can see that on July 18, 2023, the market opened at 19,787.50, which is above the previous day's high of 19,731.85. Therefore, it is not possible to take a trade using this method on July 18 because the condition is that you can use this method only if the market opens somewhere between the high and low of the previous day. Otherwise, you have to postpone using this method till the next day.

Now, on July 19, we will again create the world's simplest vertical chart -

19,850

↕

19,819.45

↕

19,690.20

↕

19,650

Now, on July 19, 2023, the market opened at 19,802.95. That means the condition was fulfilled that the market should open anywhere between the high and low of the previous day. Now we have to see whether the market takes a breakout in any direction above or below the previous day's high or low.

If the market goes above the previous day's high, then we have to sell a call with a strike price above the previous day's high at the market price and also sell a put with a strike price below the previous day's low. That means, as soon as the market started going above 19,819.45, you sold a call of 19,850 and a put of 19,650 simultaneously.

This was the breakout point towards the very top. If you do this then it is natural that after this the premium on the put of ₹ 19,650 will reduce rapidly. Then you saw that the market closed at 19,833.15. That is, even the premium on the call of ₹

19,850 could not rise appreciably. So, by creating this type of strangle, we get the benefit of reduced premium in the put and in most of the intraday, cutting such a strangle in the last half hour is always profitable.

As you have read in the previous methods, you have to keep a stop loss of maximum ₹ 2,000 in any leg and you should not sell more than 1 lot each and book whatever profit-loss is there in the last half hour of the market.

The same method has to be used in the opposite direction, too. Even if the market goes below 19,650, call of 19,850 and put of 19,650 have to be sold. In this too, as we sold at the breakout level on the lower side of the market, the premium of the call of ₹ 19,850 will start decreasing rapidly. But the put premium does not increase that much, due to which in the end, most of the deal ends in profit.

You are aware that no method of option gives you a guaranteed profit. In this method as well, you have to keep a stop loss of ₹ 2,000 per leg and you can close your position when you get reasonable profit or in the last half hour of the market.

Like any of my other methods, this method also requires you to close the deal in the last half hour. This method is very effective. To gain experience in it, you should practice paper trading for a few days. Only then you will be able to understand how you can earn a profit from it in real trading.

It is possible that some followers will be apprehensive or cautious of this method and might feel that selling at the breakout level will cause the market to rise recklessly and they will incur losses. But actually, you will see that though the premiums increase once during the breakout, but they also decrease later as the impact of the breakout subsides. Therefore, this strangle earns you profit in 80 percent of the days. It has to be used in intraday only and you should not sell more than 1 lot each.

❑

19

Summary

You have completed this Advanced Options Trading Strategies book containing my methods for earning a regular monthly income from options trading.

It is possible that after reading the book you may feel that earning money from option trading is very easy. But then you may wonder that if option trading is so simple then why has SEBI's research study found that 9 out of 10 investors book net loss in option trading?

It may also happen that when you try paper trading using the methods mentioned in this book, you may earn net profit. But when you shift from paper trade to real trade, you may incur loss. Actually, it is the tendency of human beings that the task which they consider easy during practice makes them nervous when it comes to actually performing it and they lose courage.

The same happens in option trading. When you practise paper trading, you do not have any emotional attachment with your trades. But as soon as you take a real trade, you get emotionally and mentally involved in that trade.

Since it is a matter related to money which is essential for day-to-day living and when you feel that your money is at risk in real trade, then you lose your sense of balance. As a result, you set aside the principles that you have read in the book and start trading based on your emotions, which only results in loss.

Given the context here, I would like to share with you a small incident which is true, to show how there is a pronounced or marked difference between practice and reality. My wife runs a cooking channel called 'Seema Ki Rasoi' and she is considered an expert in cooking.

I have mentioned the Bal Naga Sanyasi Mahant Shri Sahadev Giriji Maharaj in the introduction of the book. He came for my Guruji's *Bhandara* from the Aavahan Akhara in Haridwar after my Guruji died, and later, at the request of the devotees, he decided to stay back and settled at a hill there.

Both husband and wife were fascinated by the charming and magnificent appearance of Bal Sadhu. So, we made a plan to go there on a holiday and have a picnic.

I asked my wife which dessert was her speciality, which if prepared at home and served to the Mahatma would make the child in him happy.

My wife said she makes very good Balushahi. Still, to confirm, I asked her to make Balushahi first as a rehearsal so that we would know whether it was really worth serving to Sadhu Maharaj or not.

Naturally, my wife made very good, sweet and crisp Balushahi. So, we decided that during the picnic, my wife would make Balushahi on the hill itself and all the devotees from the village along with Mahatmaji would enjoy Balushahi.

We carried enough flour and ghee and other necessary ingredients so that we could make Balushahi in large quantities.

Though we had a full rehearsal (paper trade in our parlance) at home, when it was time to actually make Balushahi at Mahatmaji's ashram, my wife became nervous. My wife was used to cooking on a gas stove at home. Here, the villagers made a chulha for her with four bricks and brought her firewood. As a result, the fire would sometimes burn bright and sometimes it would be low. (Watching the ups and downs of the fire reminded me of the ups and downs in the stock market).

In the meanwhile, another great Mahant Shri Somgiri Maharaj, who is also called Peerji Maharaj by the people in the area, also arrived from another nearby ashram at Maharaj's hut along with his group to meet the newly arrived Bal Sadhu.

Mahant Shri Sahdev Giri Maharaj told him - Today some of my devotees are making Balushahi. So, you should also stay back to have the prasad.

The group of sadhus sat down, lit their chillums and waited for Balushahi.

Now my wife became even more nervous. She was not used to making such large quantities of Balushahi at a time. Therefore, all her measurements went wrong. He added too much colour to Balushahi. As the flame was inconsistent in its temperature, the Balushahi was not cooked properly. She took it out of the ghee just like that and added the syrup. Since the sugar syrup was also in large quantities, it became watery. As a result, the Balushahi looked like a lump of red flour.

Overall, the Balushahi turned out to be a failure. All the sadhus showed reluctance to eat it when they saw its colour. The great Mahant Shri Peerji Maharaj, who was present there as a guest, ordered them to consider the sincerity of the heart of the devotee and his wife and consume at least small amounts of it as prasad so that our feelings would not be hurt.

You must have realized that the sadhus only ate small pieces so as not to hurt our feelings. The villagers had already decided not to eat our Balushahi after seeing its appearance. However, on Mahantji's insistence, everyone reluctantly ate a small piece. You can imagine how my wife and I must have been in tears after seeing this happen.

The same thing can happen with you in option trading. As you know, no method of option trading is 100 percent perfect. Therefore, whenever you incur loss in any method for 2-3 consecutive days, then you can start getting worried and stop using that method altogether.

Therefore, taking small positions in real trade can prove helpful to you. For example, instead of trying to make Balushahi in large quantities at once, if my wife had made it in small quantities, she could have easily made perfect Balushahi without any issue.

Taking small positions in real trades also results in less emotional attachment and one also has the ability to tolerate small losses.

So, in essence, one should take small trades and not get emotionally attached to the trades.

The second rule is that one should take trades at different times of the day. For example, if my wife had made small quantities of Balushahi, her confidence would have increased just like the confidence that increases after booking small profits and she could have easily made perfect Balushahi for the entire group of sadhus.

Similarly, another point to remember is that if you have become an expert in a method and on most of the days, you earn from that method, then ignore the occasional losses and do not try to change the method out of fear of those occasional losses.

Because if you keep changing the methods continuously in your endless quest to find the perfect method, sometimes there will be profit and at other times there will be loss and you will be left standing at the same place from where you started.

Here too, I have another example to give. However, after reading that example, do not think that I am a supporter of fantasy cricket and after reading this example, you should not start playing fantasy cricket either. This is just an example that may help you in options trading.

Once I heard an interview of a player who had won ₹ 1 crore in fantasy cricket. In it, he said that he had deployed the same type of team for 5 years. He used to take 3 openers, front row batsmen from both the teams and 3 bowlers from the team playing first.

Because he felt that the day the first three batsmen settled down and not get out, his target would be met. His logic behind taking more bowlers for the team playing first was that there is mental pressure on the team playing later to chase the score and so, their more players get out, the benefit of which goes to the bowlers of the team batting first.

Overall, the man remained steadfast on his method for 5 years and continued to deploy the team with the same method every day. One day, the game actually worked according to his theory and he won ₹ 1 crore.

The same thing applies to option trading. If you choose your method based on logic, then keep following the same method every day. Even if there is occasional loss, you remain in overall profit throughout the month. Therefore, do not change methods repeatedly.

The final observation that I would like to make is that you should not put the book aside after reading it once, rather you should read it again and again. You will notice that every time you read it, some new creative trade setup ideas will automatically occur to you. Because I didn't write this book. The Supreme Being – the Supreme Father – the Omnipresent Being – the Supreme Soul, you may call him by whatever name you want, made me write it by making me a medium. Therefore, when you read this book again and again, that inner power will inspire your mind in the right direction, which you will definitely experience one day.

I also request you to review this book on the online platform and give me a 5-star review and write your comments. It will make me very happy.

You can also e-mail me your views at mahesh2073@yahoo.com. I am not able to respond to all e-mails. But whenever I get time, I read and mail replies to them. It is possible that your e-mail may also contain some new creative ideas, which may prove to be of some help to all the traders in the future. So, I invite you to send me your creative ideas via e-mail or YouTube comments.

I do not give my phone numbers because it is not possible to guide 2.25 lakh followers over the phone.

Finally, I conclude this book by again thanking the Almighty and praying for the well- being of all traders.

Sincerely yours,

– Mahesh Chandra Kaushik

